"Pastor Steve Austin provides a gr sickness and receive divine healing based on God's word and Steve's 25 years of experience ministering to the sick in the largest medical center in the world. This book is a must for anyone seeking to reclaim their health!"

Lisa Osteen Comes, associate pastor, Lakewood Church

"Steve Austin has offered a beautiful expression of hope in his new book, *God Heals*. His ability to bring prayer, faith, and healing together in ways that can help the reader find peace through God's healing touch is truly special. This is a must-read for anyone seeking to deepen their relationship with Christ."

Ken Carlson, MDiv, director of mission and spiritual care,
Baylor St. Luke's Medical Center, Houston

"Although the ministry of healing occurs continually through Jesus in the Gospels and again through the apostles in the book of Acts, the modern church today in Western countries has largely ignored it. Thankfully, God has raised up men like Steve Austin to reestablish the ministry of healing in the body of Christ. The church is doubly blind to its need, because it is sick but has little faith to seek Jehovah Rapha for its healing. I believe that as you read *God Heals*, your faith will soar and you will find that God is your healer, no matter what your condition."

Joan Hunter, author and evangelist;
TV host, *Miracles Happen*

"*God Heals* will help you claim the inheritance of your healing that is—and always has been—rightfully yours. With a conversational approach and an open heart, Pastor Steve makes it easy to understand that God is willing, able, and ready to heal anyone who needs it. I urge you to read this book with faith and expectation, because I know that God is still healing today."

Apostle Guillermo Maldonado, King Jesus International Ministry

"This book will bless you tremendously. Steve Austin is brilliant and knows how to pray for sick people. He visits hospitals daily and sees many miracles. I'm so glad he wrote it to help others. I salute him."

Dodie Osteen, cofounder, Lakewood Church

"As a physician, I recommend *God Heals* as an invaluable resource for anyone facing illness or disease. The principles taught in this book have the power to unlock God's healing power in your life."

Paul Osteen, MD

"The positive messaging that Pastor Steve offers is uplifting and hope filled. I appreciate his practical approach to ministry that leads to spiritual healing. I found his transparency and clarity helpful to those who read this book as a way to move toward transformation and empowerment! Absolutely loved it!"

Carla Price, elder, United Methodist Church; manager of pastoral care for a major academic medical center

GOD
heals

Eight Keys to
Defeat Sickness and
Receive Divine Healing

# STEVE AUSTIN

a division of Baker Publishing Group
Minneapolis, Minnesota

© 2023 by Stephen Austin

Published by Chosen Books
Minneapolis, Minnesota
www.chosenbooks.com

Chosen Books is a division of
Baker Publishing Group, Grand Rapids, Michigan

Printed in the United States of America

All rights reserved. No part of this publication may be reproduced, stored in a retrieval system, or transmitted in any form or by any means—for example, electronic, photocopy, recording—without the prior written permission of the publisher. The only exception is brief quotations in printed reviews.

Library of Congress Cataloging-in-Publication Data

Names: Austin, Steve, author.
Title: God heals : eight keys to defeat sickness and receive divine healing / Steve Austin.
Description: Minneapolis, Minnesota : Chosen Books, a division of Baker Publishing Group, [2023] | Includes bibliographical references.
Identifiers: LCCN 2022033176 | ISBN 9780800762803 (trade paper) | ISBN 9780800763107 (casebound) | ISBN 9781493439300 (ebook)
Subjects: LCSH: Spiritual healing—Miscellanea. | Healing—Religious aspects—Christianity—Miscellanea.
Classification: LCC BT732.5 .A97 2023 | DDC 234/.131—dc23/eng/20220829
LC record available at https://lccn.loc.gov/2022033176

Unless otherwise indicated, Scripture quotations are from the New King James Version®. Copyright © 1982 by Thomas Nelson. Used by permission. All rights reserved.

Scripture quotations identified AMP are from the Amplified® Bible (AMP), copyright © 2015 by The Lockman Foundation. Used by permission. www.Lockman.org

Scripture quotations identified AMPC are from the Amplified® Bible (AMPC), copyright © 1954, 1958, 1962, 1964, 1965, 1987 by The Lockman Foundation. Used by permission. www.Lockman.org

Scripture quotations identified CEB are from the Common English Bible. © Copyright 2011 by the Common English Bible. All rights reserved. Used by permission.

Scripture quotations identified CEV are from the Contemporary English Version © 1991, 1992, 1995 by American Bible Society. Used by permission.

Scripture quotations identified CSB are from the Christian Standard Bible®, copyright © 2017 by Holman Bible Publishers. Used by permission. Christian Standard Bible® and CSB® are federally registered trademarks of Holman Bible Publishers.

Scripture quotations identified ESV are from The Holy Bible, English Standard Version® (ESV®), copyright © 2001 by Crossway, a publishing ministry of Good News Publishers. Used by permission. All rights reserved. ESV Text Edition: 2016

Scripture quotations identified KJV are from the King James Version of the Bible.

Scripture quotations identified KJ2000 are from the King James 2000 Bible, copyright © Doctor of Theology Robert A. Couric 2000, 2003. Used by permission. All rights reserved.

Scripture quotations identified MSG are taken from *THE MESSAGE*, copyright © 1993, 2002, 2018 by Eugene H. Peterson. Used by permission of NavPress. All rights reserved. Represented by Tyndale House Publishers, Inc.

Scripture quotations identified NASB are taken from the (NASB®) New American Standard Bible®, Copyright © 1960, 1971, 1977, 1995, 2020 by The Lockman Foundation. Used by permission. All rights reserved. www.lockman.org

Scripture quotations identified NIV are from THE HOLY BIBLE, NEW INTERNATIONAL VERSION®, NIV® Copyright © 1973, 1978, 1984, 2011 by Biblica, Inc.® Used by permission. All rights reserved worldwide.

Scripture quotations identified NLT are taken from the Holy Bible, New Living Translation, copyright © 1996, 2004, 2015 by Tyndale House Foundation. Used by permission of Tyndale House Publishers, Inc., Carol Stream, Illinois 60188. All rights reserved.

Any italics in quoted material is emphasis added by the author.

Some identifying details have been changed to protect the privacy of individuals mentioned in this book.

This publication is intended to provide helpful and informative material on the subjects addressed. Readers should consult their personal health professionals before adopting any of the suggestions in this book or drawing inferences from it. The author and publisher expressly disclaim responsibility for any adverse effects arising from the use or application of the information contained in this book.

Author represented by Dupree/Miller & Associates

Baker Publishing Group publications use paper produced from sustainable forestry practices and post-consumer waste whenever possible.

23 24 25 26 27 28 29 7 6 5 4 3 2 1

This book is dedicated to everyone
who needs healing in their body or soul,
their families, and the health-care professionals
who work tirelessly to help them heal.
God is with you!

# Contents

# Foreword

LAKEWOOD CHURCH IS LOCATED less than five miles from the Texas Medical Center, the largest medical center in the world. Over the years, thousands of medical patients from around the world and their families have come to Lakewood for prayer and encouragement. Many, if not most, have an unfavorable doctor's report and oftentimes feel as if there is little hope. I encourage them to have faith, pray often, and believe their healing is coming. I'm telling you what I tell each of them: God can show up in an instant and change everything for you.

There are many biblical stories where the heroes of faith believed God for a victory and did not waver from that belief. They spoke words of victory and praised God for it even before they saw it. They viewed their battle through eyes of faith and spoke words of triumph even when others around them spoke defeat. They didn't listen to the naysayers or focus on their trouble, but instead focused on the One who is bigger than the danger they faced: Jehovah Rapha—God, their Healer.

Almost all of us will face a life-threatening situation, such as a medical condition or disease. It is how we respond to it that makes the greatest difference. That is why I think this book, *God Heals*, by my friend Steve Austin is important. Steve is a valuable member of our staff at Lakewood and has a heart for those facing illness. He has helped thousands of people over the years, and I can think of no one better to author this book.

*God Heals* is well written, easy to read, and expertly organized. Steve helps you to believe that God is your Healer, and to understand the significance of your faith and how it affects the words you speak and the prayers you pray. This book will help you to appreciate the power found in praise and equip you with God's promises as you persevere.

I encourage you to dig deeply into God's Word as you confront your challenges, and to seek out those who speak God's promises into your life. Steve is such a person. Read each page of *God Heals* with anticipation and an open heart and allow this book to speak the healing Word of God into your life. God bless you.

Joel Osteen

# Acknowledgments

NO ONE DOES ANYTHING GREAT in life without the help of many people. I want to acknowledge and give my deepest thanks to some of the people who made this book possible.

To Jesus Christ, my Lord and Savior: Thank You for saving me, loving me unconditionally, and seeing the best in me. Apart from You, I can do nothing. I give You all praise, glory, and honor.

To Suzie, my amazing Proverbs 31 wife: Thank you for your unfailing love and constant support and encouragement. Besides Jesus, you are my greatest blessing and the wind beneath my wings.

To my precious daughters, Lindsey and Lauren: You are unique and wonderful masterpieces. I am so proud of you and honored to be your dad. Thank you for always loving me and cheering me on.

To my mother, Sandy, who is with Jesus: Thank you for being the most loving, supportive mother imaginable and a great role model. You will always be in my heart and inspire me.

To my pastors, Joel and Victoria Osteen: Thank you for your love and support for 23 years, for being such amazing role models, and for the treasures of wisdom, encouragement, and inspiration you have poured into me. I wouldn't be who I am today without your influence.

To Shannon Marvin: Thank you not only for being the best agent on the planet, but for being a friend. I am beyond grateful for your skillful representation, wisdom, and guidance that made this process so easy and positioned *God Heals* to impact maximum lives. Thank you to the rest of the team at Dupree/Miller, all of whom were amazing and such a joy to work with.

To Kim Bangs: Thank you for believing in me, seeing the value of this book, and being the best editor I could possibly have had. *God Heals* would not be what it is without your leadership and wisdom. I am forever grateful! Thank you to Natasha Sperling, Dan Pitts, Deirdre Close, Rebecca Schriner, Mycah Gavic, and the rest of the team at Baker Publishing. I can't express in words how wonderful you were to work with and how much I appreciate the excellent work you put into this project. You are the best!

To Mama Dodie Osteen, a living legend: Thank you for being one of the greatest examples of Christlike love and compassion. You are an incredible inspiration to me.

To Misty Gonzalez: Thank you for your loving friendship. This book would not be what it is without your contribution.

To Janet McCauley: Thank you for your support that made this book possible.

# Introduction

I'VE HEARD IT SAID that life is 10 percent what happens to us and 90 percent how we respond to what happens to us. Sickness may have happened to you or your loved one, but I want to help you respond in a way that will help you win the battle. The eight keys I share in this book are based on the Word of God—which never fails—and 25 years of experience ministering to thousands of sick people in the largest medical center in the world (the Texas Medical Center in Houston, Texas).

Chapters 1 through 8 focus on these keys: (1) knowing God as Healer, (2) unleashing the power of faith, (3) utilizing the miracle in your mouth, (4) praying prayers that work, (5) praise preceding the victory, (6) healing your soul, (7) winning the invisible battle, and (8) taking care of your temple.

Although I can't guarantee results, these keys have worked for countless people. The apostle Paul wrote, "Thus I fight: not as one who beats the air" (1 Corinthians 9:26). With these keys, you won't fight your sickness as one who beats the air. You will be equipped to win.

Getting diagnosed with a serious medical condition can bring sudden and dramatic changes to a person's life. They get thrown into a spin cycle of doctors' visits, tests, treatments, and hospital stays, often fighting for their very lives. Many patients have told me they feel like they're on a roller coaster. In the midst of this upheaval and turmoil, even the strongest Christians can lose their spiritual footing. Many are also separated from their normal support system and don't receive adequate spiritual care. The Scripture says, "The spirit of a man will sustain him in sickness" (Proverbs 18:14). You have to be proactive about keeping your spirit strong. This book is designed to help you do just that. I have included healing Scriptures, prayers, daily declarations, and many real-life testimonies to strengthen your spirit, encourage your faith, and help you reclaim your health.

## Get Your Hopes Up!

I have been in the trenches with countless patients and their families, and I know how rough battling a serious illness can be. Maybe you started out with a lot of hope, but you or your loved one has been sick for a while, you feel battle weary, and your hope is hanging on by a thread. I want to stir you up again to believe God for your miracle. No matter what your situation looks like, no matter what the doctors told you or what you read on Google about your condition, there is always hope with God. He is the God of all hope (Romans 15:13). He has *all* power. He can do the impossible. He spoke worlds into existence, parted the Red Sea, and raised Jesus from the dead. The Scripture says, "He does great things too marvelous to understand. He performs countless miracles" (Job 9:10 NLT).

Your situation is never hopeless with God. It's not too big for Him. It's not too far gone. It's not too late. One touch from God can change everything. You are God's child, and He loves you more than you can imagine. He wants the best for you. He wants you healthy. If God was done with you, He would have already taken you home. As long as you have breath in your lungs, God has a purpose for your life. The doctors don't have the final say; God does. Nothing is over until God says it's over. Get your hopes up! Dare to believe God! Zechariah 9:12 says, "Return to the stronghold, you prisoners of hope." Don't be a prisoner of negativity, doubt, or fear. Be a prisoner of hope.

That medical condition may look big and scary, but our God is *bigger* and *stronger*. That sickness may look like it has power over you, but God has *all* power. It may look like you are surrounded by sickness and challenges, but God is surrounding what is surrounding you. You may not see a way, but God always has a way. Hope in Him!

Having hope is how you release your faith. The Scripture says, "Faith is the substance of things *hoped for*" (Hebrews 11:1). You can't have faith without first having hope. Hope is the oxygen of faith. It is more than just wishing. It is a *confident expectation*. Do you confidently expect God to heal you? If you don't now, I believe you will after reading this book.

Hope also means having a positive attitude. As I interviewed many people for this book who received healing from cancer and other diseases, almost everyone said the number one thing they would tell people battling an illness is "Stay positive." No matter what you are facing, you can decide today to be positive and hopeful, knowing that God is on the throne and has you in the palm of His hand.

## God Is with You

As you journey toward your healing, you may not always feel God. You may not be able to figure out what He's up to. I've learned that God works the most when we see and feel Him the least. That's what faith is all about. If you can see it, feel it, or figure it out, you don't need faith. You may wonder at times if God even sees what you are going through or cares. Let me assure you that God cares about you more than you can comprehend. You are His beloved child. His eyes are always on you, and He is with you every step of the way. You are not in this battle alone.

The Scripture says God will never leave you nor forsake you (Hebrews 13:5). In Psalm 23:4 (NLT), David said, "Even when I walk through the darkest valley, I will not be afraid, *for you are close beside me*. Your rod and your staff protect and comfort me." We all walk through some valleys, but God is close beside us in the valleys of life. His rod and staff protect and comfort us. After this verse about walking through a valley, the next verse says, "You prepare a table for me in the presence of my enemies" (Psalm 23:5). God has a table prepared for you on the other side of this sickness. It's a table of health, freedom, and victory!

Jesus said, "My Father is always working" (John 5:17 NLT). God is always working for His children. The Scripture says He never sleeps nor slumbers (Psalm 121:4). I am in hospitals ministering to sick people all the time, and I constantly see God working and doing miracles. Sometimes it is an awe-inspiring, divine healing. I lost count a long time ago of all the tumors I've seen vanish and people miraculously healed when the doctors said there was nothing more they could do. Sometimes, God causes an appointment to open with the doctor you wanted when they said they were booked for months. Sometimes, it is amazing people God sends to help, care for, and encourage you. God works in all kinds of ways, big and small, every day. Recently, there was a woman who urgently needed a heart transplant, and her doctor, a world-renowned heart transplant surgeon, said that based on genetic makeup and other factors, the odds were infinitesimally small of her finding a matching heart. She needed a miracle to survive. Despite impossible odds, God came through at the last minute, and she received a matching heart! The day after her surgery, she was sitting up in bed talking as if nothing had ever happened. No matter what you are facing, don't ever count God out. The odds may be against you, but the Most High God is for you. He will never let you down!

## Work with God

There are two parts to faith—God's part and our part. God will not fail to do His part, but we have to do our part. Every time a miracle or healing was done in the Bible, somebody had to do something. God told Moses to stretch out his staff before He parted the Red Sea (Exodus 14:15–16, 21). The widow had to gather up empty vessels before God multiplied her oil (2 Kings 4:1–7). Naaman had to dip in the Jordan River seven times to be healed of leprosy (2 Kings 5:10–14). Peter had to get out of the boat to walk on water (Matthew 14:28–29). The lepers had to go show themselves to the priests before they were healed (Luke 17:12–14). The boy had to give his five loaves and two fish to Jesus before He multiplied them and fed the five thousand (Matthew 14:13–21). The purpose of this book is to help you do your part so you can receive your healing. When you give God something to work with by applying the keys in this book, you are going to see God do supernatural things in your life.

## First Things First

I know you picked up this book because you or your loved one needs healing, but there is something even more important than that—your eternal destiny. A physical healing may last a lifetime, but your eternal destiny is forever. With this in mind, I want to ask you an important question: If you died today, do you know beyond any doubt where you would spend eternity? If not, I want to invite you to secure your eternal destiny right now before you go any further.

God made it so easy. He sent Jesus to die on the cross for our sins so they would no longer separate us from God and we could enjoy eternal life with Him in heaven. John 3:16 says, "For God so loved the world that He gave His only begotten Son, that whoever believes in Him should not perish but have everlasting life." Salvation does not depend on how good of a person you are or how many good deeds you've done. It is a free gift from God that only comes through faith in Jesus Christ. The Scripture says, "For by grace you have been saved through faith, and that not of yourselves; it is the gift of God, not of works, lest anyone should boast" (Ephesians 2:8–9).

If you have never asked Jesus to be your Lord and Savior, or if you would like to rededicate your life to Him, I invite you to pray the prayer below and receive the free gift of salvation. Don't put it off. The Bible says, "*Today* is the day of salvation" (2 Corinthians 6:2 NLT). Tomorrow is not guaranteed.

#### *Prayer of Salvation or Rededication*

*Jesus, I believe You died on the cross for my sins and eternal salvation is found in You alone. I ask You to come into my heart and be my Lord and Savior. I give You my life and desire to follow You the rest of my days. Thank You for saving me and making me part of God's family. In Your precious name I pray, Amen.*

If you prayed that simple prayer, the Bible says you have been born again spiritually. You are guaranteed not only eternal life with God in heaven, but a treasure trove of promises and benefits in this life, including healing. So read on . . . your healing awaits.

1

KEY 1

# God Is a Healer

I am the LORD who heals you.

Exodus 15:26

Let it be a settled fact: It is God's will to heal you.

T. L. Osborne

IF YOU OR A LOVED ONE NEEDS HEALING, I have great news: We serve a healing God! In Exodus 15:26, He said, "I am the LORD who heals you." He connected His very name and identity to healing. Healing is not just something God does; *it is who He is*. He is not just our God and our Lord and Savior; *He is our Healer*. He healed people throughout the Bible, and He still heals today. He never changes. I have personally seen hundreds of miraculous healings of virtually every sickness and disease over the last 25 years. Whatever you are facing today, it's not too big for our God. He has not only the power but the desire to heal you. You are His child, and He loves you more than you can fathom. He wants you to be healthy and flourish.

I grew up in churches that did not teach anything about healing. For the first thirty years of my life, it never entered my mind that God heals. I was a young, healthy attorney, and the topic of healing was not on my radar. One day, I was invited to a luncheon for Christian professionals, and the speaker was an evangelist who held large healing crusades all over the world. He told how God is still in the healing business and described some of the many miracles at his crusades. I was dubious, but after he vividly described several amazing miracles, I was intrigued. I thought, *If this is real, I want to see it with my own eyes.* After his message, I introduced myself and told him I would like to go on one of his trips.

A couple of months later, I accompanied him to India on my first foreign mission trip, mostly out of curiosity. A natural skeptic and trained as a lawyer to base everything on facts and evidence, I was, you might say, a doubting Thomas. I even hired a videographer to document any healings that took place. I wanted documentary proof. What I experienced on that trip changed me forever. It was a major catalyst for me leaving the legal profession and going into full-time ministry the following year. I saw with my own eyes people instantly healed of blindness, deafness, paralysis, cancer, and many other conditions. All my left-brain thinking and the religious box I had put God in were shattered forever. God is so much bigger than our religion.

Jesus said, "These signs will follow those who believe: In My name . . . they will lay hands on the sick and they *will* recover" (Mark 16:17–18). I took Him at His Word, and for the first time laid my hands on sick people and watched God do miracles. One man was paralyzed on the left side of his body from a stroke and could not raise his arm at all. After

I prayed over him, he was able to freely lift his arm above his head and praise God. Then I met a woman who had been in a wheelchair for many years. I could see that her legs were rail thin and atrophied from lack of use. After I laid hands on her and commanded healing in the name of Jesus the way Jesus and His disciples modeled for us in the Bible, she got up from her wheelchair and started walking. She was wobbly at first, but as she lifted her hands and started praising God, she grew stronger with every step. We held healing crusades in the morning and evening for ten days, and there were countless more undeniable healings. Medical doctors on hand confirmed every one. CT scans conducted on people with cancer after the crusades showed that tumors had vanished in many. After that trip, I would never again doubt God's healing power.

It took three flights and 36 hours from that remote part of India to get back home, and I had a lot of time to process what I had experienced. I had a conversation with God that went something like this: "God, that was incredible. I've never seen anything like that. But why did I have to travel eight thousand miles to the other side of the world to see that? Why don't I see more miracles like that in America?" The Lord's reply was quick and clear in my spirit: *It is because in America, people put more faith in doctors, information, and technology. They read something on Google about their condition or hear something from a doctor, and that becomes their truth. They believe that instead of believing Me.* He also showed me that most churches don't teach about healing and don't encourage faith for healing and miracles, so most people don't believe for it. It was an enlightening conversation, and God used it to light a fire in me to educate people about His healing power. I encourage you to put your faith in God for your healing. God uses doctors, medicine, and technology, but ultimately He is your Healer, and He is not limited to those resources.

After returning home, I prayed for every sick person I encountered, and God continued doing miracles. One day I got a call to come and pray for a young man who had cancer in the base of his brain and spinal column. Doctors had sent him home saying there was nothing more they could do. Often, God does His greatest work when man gets to the end of himself because that's when He alone gets the glory. I laid hands on that young man and fervently prayed with every ounce of faith I had. A week or so later, he was given an MRI that showed every trace of cancer had vanished from his body. That was over twenty years ago, and he is still alive and thriving today. Since that time, I have seen God heal hundreds of people—some instantly and others over time. I don't claim to have the gift of healing; I am just a regular person whose eyes were opened about the healing power of God and who began exercising my faith in this area. I don't know what your religious background is, but I'm here to tell you with absolute confidence: God is a healing God!

## The God Who Heals You

As I've ministered to thousands of sick people over the last 25 years, I've discovered that people have all kinds of erroneous beliefs about God when it comes to healing. Some have actually been taught that God puts sickness on people, or at least allows it, to teach them a lesson. This is completely false. There were times in the Old Testament when God put sicknesses and diseases *on His enemies*, but ever since the age of grace began, when Jesus died on the cross, God has not put sickness on people for any reason.

Sickness and disease occur for three reasons: (1) we have fallen bodies that can sometimes be vulnerable to sickness; (2) we live in a fallen world, where there are toxins, viruses, and other pernicious elements that can cause disease; and (3) we have a spiritual enemy who sometimes attacks people's bodies with sickness. (I will discuss this last source more in chapter 7.) But one thing is certain: *Sickness and disease are not from God.*

Other people have been taught that God no longer heals today, that such miracles were only for the time of Jesus. This is also completely false and easily disproven by the Bible and the countless healings happening every day all over the world. What you believe about God will determine how you make it through your sickness. You have to know that God is a loving, merciful, healing God.

**What you *believe* about God will determine *how* you make it through your sickness.**

God revealed Himself as our Healer early in the Bible when He told the Israelites, "I am the LORD who heals you" (Exodus 15:26). By starting with the words "I am," He was saying, "Healing is not just something I do; it is who I am. Healing is part of My nature." In the original Hebrew language, this translates as the name *Jehovah Rapha* (RAH-fah)—"the God who heals you." I encourage you to incorporate the name Jehovah Rapha into your prayers when you pray for healing. By doing so, you are calling on God as your Healer and invoking His miracle-working power. Pray like this:

*Father God, I thank You that You are Jehovah Rapha, the God who heals me. Healing is not just something You do; it is who You are. You connected Your very name and identity to healing. I ask You to touch me now and heal my body everywhere I need it. Remove every trace of [name your affliction], sickness, infection, and pain from my body. Completely restore my health and make me whole, in Jesus' mighty name, Amen.*

A few chapters after God revealed Himself as our Healer, He told the Israelites, "I will take sickness away from the midst of you" (Exodus 23:25). That is a promise from Almighty God, who never lies or fails. He will take sickness from the midst of you. Healing is God's heart for you. After Moses was given the revelation of God as our Healer, he lived in perfect health until the age of 120. The Bible says his eyes never grew dim and his natural vigor never diminished (Deuteronomy 34:7). There is power when we gain the revelation of all that God is and all that He can do in our lives.

David gave us another revelation about the healing nature of God when he wrote in Psalm 103:2–3, "Forget not all His benefits . . . who heals all your diseases." In this verse, God tells us that healing is one of His benefits. He even exhorts us not to forget it. He says He heals *all* our diseases, not just some. That is a promise from God you can hold on to and have total confidence in. God never breaks His word.

I have great respect for doctors and medicine, but our fate does not depend on them. God uses doctors and medicine, but healing comes from Him. They are limited; He is not. He created the universe with the words of His mouth. He said, "Let there be," and everything formed out of nothing. He parted the Red Sea. He rained manna from heaven. He protected the three Hebrew boys in the fiery furnace, and they emerged unharmed, without even the smell of smoke. He multiplied five loaves and two fish so they fed more than five thousand people. He raised Jesus from the dead after three days. Job 9:10 (NIV) says, "He performs wonders that cannot be fathomed, miracles that cannot be counted." God is bigger and more powerful than we can comprehend. Your sickness may look big and scary, but it's no match for our God. If you are in the hospital, look at the machines, monitors, tubes, and IVs in your room and say, "My God is bigger than this." When you look at your sickness in light of the overwhelming bigness and power of God, it will change your perspective. Don't focus on the sickness; focus on God.

**Don't focus on the *sickness*; focus on *God*.**

**"I Want To"**

Maybe it's easy for you to believe God has the power to heal you, but you struggle with whether He really *wants* to. Perhaps you feel unworthy to receive a miracle from God or think He doesn't care much about you. These are common lies the enemy plants in people's minds to prevent them from receiving their healing. I want you to know for sure that God not only has the power to heal you; *He wants to*.

When Jesus came to the earth, He revealed God to us in a very tangible way. The Scripture says He was "the visible image of the invisible God" (Colossians 1:15 NLT). He said, "If you've seen Me, you've seen the Father" (John 14:9, paraphrased). Everything Jesus said and did revealed the nature of God. One of the main things He did was heal the sick. In fact, *every* person who came to Jesus for healing got healed. Multitudes were healed of every kind of sickness and disease. *No one was turned away*. Matthew 12:15 says, "Great multitudes followed Him, and *He healed them all*." Matthew 14:36 says, "As many as touched [Him] were made perfectly whole." Matthew 15:30 (NLT) says, "A vast crowd brought to him people who were lame, blind, crippled, those who couldn't speak, and many others. They laid them before Jesus, and *he healed them all*." Acts 10:38 says, "God anointed Jesus of Nazareth with the Holy Spirit and with power, who went about doing good and healing *all* who were oppressed by the devil, for God was with Him." Thirteen times in Scripture, it says Jesus healed them *all*. He never denied anyone healing. Jesus showed us beyond any doubt that God is our Healer, and He still heals today. Hebrews 13:8 says that "Jesus Christ is the same yesterday, today, and forever." He never changes. There wasn't a day of miracles, as some churches teach. We serve a God of miracles. Healing and miracles are part of His nature.

Mark 1:40–42 (MSG) says, "A leper came to [Jesus], begging on his knees, 'If you want to, you can cleanse me.' Deeply moved, Jesus put out his hand, touched him, and said, '*I want to*. Be clean.' Then and there the leprosy was gone, his skin smooth and healthy." Those three words "*I want to*" summarize God's heart toward you. He wants to heal you. We serve an *I want to* God. Maybe you think He's too busy to be concerned with your sickness, that you haven't lived a good enough life, or that He doesn't really care about you, but nothing could be further from the truth. God is saying to you today, "*I want to*." He is your heavenly Father, and you are His child. No father wants to see their child sick, and God is the best Father of all. He wants nothing but the best for you. He said in 3 John 2, "Beloved, I *wish above all things* that you prosper and *be in good health*, even as your soul prospers." God wants you to be healed so much, He sacrificed His only Son for your healing.

## Jesus Paid for Your Healing

A foundational truth of Christianity that most Christians are not taught is that healing was part of Jesus' atoning work on the cross. Before Adam and Eve sinned in the Garden, there was no sickness, disease, or pain. Sickness and death entered the world because of sin. Even after the Fall, Adam lived 930 years, Methuselah lived 969 years, and most people lived many hundreds of years because the ravages of sin on the world and the body had not yet taken full effect. When Jesus died on the cross, He not only paid the price for our sins, but for everything that came into the world as a result of sin. The Bible says He took all our sicknesses and infirmities upon Himself and paid the price with His life for us to have divine health.

Isaiah 53:4–5 (CSB) says, "Yet *he himself bore our sicknesses*, and he carried our pains . . . and *we are healed by his wounds*." This verse was a prophecy about Jesus written eight hundred years before He died on the cross. It foretold that He would die not only for our sins but for our sicknesses as well. Some of this verse's meaning was lost when it was translated from the original Hebrew language to English. Here is the verse's meaning in the original Hebrew: "Surely He has borne our diseases, sicknesses, and maladies, has healed us and made us completely whole . . . and by His stripes we are healed."[1] Two verses in the New Testament that were written after Jesus' death quote this verse from Isaiah and confirm its meaning. Matthew 8:17 says, "He Himself took our infirmities and bore our sicknesses." The word *infirmities* in this verse means sicknesses, diseases and weakness. First Peter 2:24 says, "By [His] stripes you were healed." *Stripes* refers to the lacerations Jesus took on His body when He was beaten. These verses tell us that Jesus suffered in His body so we wouldn't have to. Notice how they are written in the past tense: He *took* our infirmities. He *bore* our sicknesses. By His stripes we *were* healed. He's not waiting to heal us at some point in the future. He already healed us when He took our sicknesses and diseases on Himself at the cross. Jesus paid the price for our healing two thousand years ago with His precious blood. You may be waiting for your healing to manifest, but biblically and spiritually *it is already a done deal. In God's reality, you are not a sick person trying to get well; you are a healthy person resisting sickness.*

If all you have been taught and all you have believed is that Jesus died just for your sins, you are missing out on your full package of salvation benefits. *Jesus did not die on the cross just to give us a ticket to heaven while leaving us sick, broken, and defeated on earth.* God did not give us His very best by sacrificing His only Son on the cross to then say, "I'm sorry, you just have to live with that sickness." No, that doesn't make sense, and that's not what the Bible teaches. In fact, the word for "saved" in the original Greek of the New Testament is the word *sozo* (Strong's 4982). This word occurs in verses like "For by grace you have been saved" (Ephesians 2:8), "There is no other name under heaven given among men by which we must be saved" (Acts 4:12), and other verses about our salvation in Christ. The word *sozo* encompasses much more than our eternal salvation. One of the meanings of *sozo* is "to save one suffering from disease, to make well, heal, restore to health." It is clear from Scripture that *healing was part of Christ's atoning work on the cross and part of our salvation benefits package.* Your healing is like your salvation: It is a free gift paid for by the blood of Jesus. All you have to do is receive it by faith.

You might wonder, *If Jesus took my sicknesses, why am I sick?* Great question. Just because God promises us something does not mean it is automatic. The promises of God don't just fall on us. We play a big part in receiving His promises. God gave the Israelites the Promised Land, but they still had to rise up, enter in, and possess it by faith—and there were giants in the land they had to defeat along the way. They had to do their part. It's the same for us when it comes to receiving the promises of God in our lives. Just because God promises us something doesn't mean He's going to deliver it to us on a silver platter with no effort on our part. If He gave us everything that way, we would never grow in our character and faith. We also have an enemy who is not going to roll out the red carpet for us. He hates when people get healed supernaturally and God gets the glory for it. We must fight to see the promises of God manifested in our lives. We have to dig our heels in, refuse to give up, and show the enemy we are more determined than he is. I will discuss our battle with the enemy and how it relates to your healing in chapter 7.

## You Are Worthy

Over the years, I've had many sick people confess to me that they don't feel worthy to receive healing from God because of their past sins or because they don't feel like they've lived a good enough life. My own mother struggled with feelings of unworthiness as she battled her disease. It is one of the enemy's favorite lies. He knows if he can get you to focus on your own guilt and shame instead of what Jesus did for you on the cross, it will be almost impossible to receive your healing. How can a person receive from God when they feel so unworthy? If you don't think you are worthy to receive a miracle from God, you won't have the faith to receive one. I want to eliminate that lie from your mind forever.

At the cross, Jesus paid the full penalty of our sins—past, present, and future. Not only did He take our sins upon Himself, but He gave us His righteousness. We can't earn it, and we don't deserve it; it is a free gift of grace. The Scripture says, "For He [God] made Him [Jesus] who knew no sin to be sin for us, *that we might become the righteousness of God in Him*" (2 Corinthians 5:21). Because of what Jesus did for us on the cross, we who are in Christ became the righteousness of God. You don't get any more righteous than that! There is no longer any sin issue separating us from God. When God looks at you, He doesn't see your sins, mistakes, and failures. He sees you as totally righteous and blameless because of the blood of Jesus. God has already forgiven you. You are completely worthy, loved, accepted, and approved by Almighty God, not because of anything you did, but because of what Jesus did. When Jesus was baptized by John the Baptist, the voice of God the Father boomed from heaven, "This is My beloved Son, in whom I am well pleased." Your heavenly Father is saying the same thing to you: "You are My beloved child, in whom I am well pleased."

I once ministered to a man who had cancer in several places in his body. He was scheduled for his first surgery in a couple of days and wanted to speak to a chaplain. With tears, he shared that he felt unworthy to receive God's forgiveness, love, and healing because of the life he had lived. I told him what I just told you—that Jesus Christ made him worthy. Once he got that revelation and was set free from guilt, shame, and condemnation, he was able to receive from God. Over the following months, he had some powerful personal encounters with God, and one by one the tumors began to disappear from his body. Even the doctors admitted it was a miracle! When he started focusing on the goodness, mercy, and grace of God and let go of any feelings of unworthiness, it opened the door for God to move in his life.

I pray the same for you. Reject forever any thoughts of unworthiness or guilt. You don't have to earn God's approval.

Jesus already took care of that for you. Rest in the finished work of the cross.

## God Loves You

Sometimes when we go through a difficult or prolonged illness, the enemy whispers in our minds, *Where is God? If He loves you, why is He letting you go through this?* He will try to convince you God doesn't love you or care about you. That is a lie. You are God's child, and He loves you fervently and unconditionally. God is not mad at you; He is madly in love with you. He loves you so much, He sacrificed His only Son for you. The Scripture says, "See what great love the Father has lavished on us, that we should be called children of God!" (1 John 3:1 NIV). He calls you "beloved" 42 times in the New Testament. The Scripture says His banner over you is love (Song of Solomon 2:4). I want you to imagine a banner over your head that says, "Loved and approved by Almighty God."

The evidence that God loves us is not living a problem-free life. Nobody has a problem-free life. The apostle Paul was beaten, stoned, and left for dead, shipwrecked three times, imprisoned several times, bitten by a poisonous snake, and suffered many other hardships—all while doing his best to serve God. He confessed that at times he "despaired even of life" (2 Corinthians 1:8). Yet, in the midst of all these trials, he wrote, "I am persuaded that neither death nor life, nor angels nor principalities nor powers, nor things present nor things to come, nor height nor depth, nor any other created thing, shall be able to separate us from the love of God which is in Christ Jesus our Lord" (Romans 8:38–39). Nothing can ever separate you from the love of God. He promised He would never leave you nor forsake you (Hebrews 13:5). He's not just with you on the mountaintop; He's with you in the valleys of life. In the dark times, He carries you in His arms even when you don't realize it, like in the poem "Footprints in the Sand." Psalm 68:19 (NLT) says, "Praise the Lord; praise God our savior! For each day he carries us in his arms." Rest in His loving arms. He's got you.

## When Healing Doesn't Come

Maybe you are thinking that all this sounds encouraging, but, like me, you have known people or had a loved one who did not get healed of an illness, despite having great faith and doing everything they knew to do. I wrote this book on healing, but my own mother died after an eight-year battle with dementia. I did everything I talk about in this book to help her receive healing, but God had a different plan. I have ministered to thousands of sick people for 25 years and witnessed countless awe-inspiring miracles, but I have also seen many faith-filled people not receive healing this side of heaven. I don't pretend to have all the answers. We will never know all the reasons some people get miraculously healed and others do not. But I want to share a few thoughts on the matter.

One reason not everyone gets healed on earth is because God is sovereign and He has an individual plan for each person's life. We may not always know or understand the plan. We may not agree with the plan. But God always has the best plan. He also has an eternal perspective. We get so fixated on this life and this world, but God has a bigger, eternal view. He looks at things differently than we do. He said, "My thoughts are not your thoughts, nor are your ways My ways. . . . For as the heavens are higher than the earth, so are My ways higher than your ways, and My thoughts higher than your thoughts" (Isaiah 55:8–9).

God gave us the biblical keys to healing I share in this book so we could do our part to receive divine healing, not to control Him. We play a vital role, but at the end of the day, He determines the final outcome. And we're not always going to understand that outcome. We can't want a certain outcome so badly that it becomes an idol and supplants the will of God in our hearts and lives. In the end, we must endeavor to be like Jesus, who said, "Abba, Father, all things are possible for You. Take this cup away from Me; nevertheless, not what I will, but what You will" (Mark 14:36). I believe it is always God's will to heal, but He does it His way and on His timetable. Sometimes He heals instantly, sometimes over time, and sometimes the ultimate way—by taking someone home to heaven.

God does not favor people who get healed on earth. He loves all His children equally and has no favorites. As proof of this, some of the most important people in the Bible did not receive healing on earth. Elisha, one of the greatest prophets who ever lived, did many astonishing miracles, including raising a boy from the dead. He did more miracles than anyone else in the Old Testament. Even after his death, Elisha's bones still had so much power and anointing in them that when a dead man was lowered into his tomb and touched his bones, he came back to life! (2 Kings 13:20–21). Yet the Bible says Elisha himself became sick and died of his illness (2 Kings 13:14).

David was the greatest king Israel ever had. God called him a man after His own heart. He wrote most of the Psalms and was a direct ancestor of Jesus. If anybody had special favor with God, it was David. When his baby became deathly ill, David prayed, fasted, and lay on the ground all night pleading with God. But God chose to take the baby home to heaven. David did not get bitter and fall away from God.

He picked himself up and went to the temple to worship (2 Samuel 12:20). He said, "I will go to him [when I die], but he will not return to me" (2 Samuel 12:23 AMP). David knew where his baby had gone and that he would be reunited with him again one day for all eternity, never to be separated again. That's why the Bible says believers do not grieve as those who have no hope. We grieve, but we do so with the hope of eternal life in Christ Jesus. Jesus said, "Whoever lives and believes in Me *shall never die*" (John 11:26). Believers in Christ never really die; we just transition from this life into a far more glorious, eternal life.

The apostle Paul, who wrote half the New Testament and did many amazing miracles, had what he described as a "thorn in the flesh" (2 Corinthians 12:7). Many Bible scholars believe Paul was referring to a physical infirmity, specifically that he was legally blind. Paul wrote to the Galatians, "You know that *because of physical infirmity* I preached the gospel to you at the first . . . if possible, *you would have plucked out your own eyes and given them to me*" (Galatians 4:13–15). He later wrote, "See with what large letters I have written to you with my own hand!" (Galatians 6:11). He likely wrote in large letters because of his poor eyesight. The Scripture says he prayed three times for God to remove this thorn in the flesh, but God did not. He told Paul, "My grace is sufficient for you" (2 Corinthians 12:9). Rather than heal Paul, God gave him the grace to endure the infirmity. Certainly, Paul was not lacking in faith, nor was he doing anything wrong that prevented his healing. He gave everything he had to serve God faithfully, even while he suffered in many ways. Not only was Paul not healed, but he was also unable to help one of his close friends and helpers get healed: "Trophimus I have left in Miletus sick" (2 Timothy 4:20).

The moral of these stories is this: We do our part, but God is sovereign. Sometimes we don't get the results we are hoping for, but it doesn't mean we did anything wrong, that God is uncaring, or that He has let us down. It just means He had a different plan than ours. And we have to be at peace with that, even when we don't understand it. We have to let God be God.

Another reason not everyone gets healed on earth is because this world is not our home and our life here is temporary. The Scripture compares our life on earth to a vapor or wisp of air (Psalm 39:5; James 4:14). We are just passing through this earth for a brief time before returning to our eternal home in heaven. David wrote that God has given each of us our own set number of days on this earth: "All the days ordained for me were written in your book before one of them came to be" (Psalm 139:16 NIV). Sometimes the number of days God ordained for a person's life has been fulfilled, and it is just their time to go home.

Hebrews 11 is often called the "Hall of Faith" chapter because it defines what faith is and lists many heroes of faith in the Bible—people like Noah, Abraham, Moses, David, and others. Verse 13 says, "All these people were still living by faith when they died. They did not receive the things promised; they only saw them and welcomed them from a distance, admitting that they were foreigners and strangers on earth" (NIV). These giants of the faith stayed in faith until their last breath. They did not receive all the promises of God in this lifetime, but they kept a good attitude because they recognized that this earth was not their home, and they were just passing through. Like them, our attitude should be: *No matter what happens, I am going to have faith until I draw my last breath. I am going to totally trust God, whether things go my way or not.*

The good news is, *whether we get healed on earth or by going to heaven, we win!* If we get healed on earth, it's a win. If we depart from this world and go to be with Jesus, it's an even bigger win. The apostle Paul wrote, "For to me, to live is Christ and *to die is gain*. . . . I am torn between the two: I desire to depart and be with Christ, which is *better by far*" (Philippians 1:21, 23 NIV). He said to die is actually *gain*; to depart and be with Christ is not just a little better, but *better by far*. There is no sickness or disease in heaven. No sorrow, trials, or stress in heaven. No conflict or crime in heaven. Only unspeakable joy. This world can't begin to compare. When we break the chains of this earthly tent and go to be with Jesus, it will be the most victorious day of our lives.

So here is my encouragement to you before we move on to the next chapters. Use the eight keys to healing in this book to the best of your ability. Have faith that God is a miracle-working, healing God and that nothing is impossible with Him. At the same time, put yourself or your loved one in His loving arms and trust Him with the final outcome, whatever that may be. No one loves you or your loved one more than God. He has you in the palm of His hand, and He has the best plan for your life.

KEY 2

# Unleashing the Power of Faith

> If you can believe, all things are possible to him who believes.
>
> Mark 9:23

> God is not limited by the facts. He's a supernatural God.
>
> Joel Osteen

GOD HAS GIVEN YOU EVERY KEY you need to receive healing. By far the most powerful—and the one that undergirds all other keys—is your faith. Faith connects you to the unlimited, miracle-working power of Almighty God and makes the impossible possible. Jesus said, "If you can believe, all things are possible to him who believes" (Mark 9:23). Not some things. Not most things. *All* things are possible if you can believe God for it. He didn't say if you can figure it out, if you are a good enough person, or if you beg Him enough. He said *just believe.*

If you have been battling a serious illness, especially a prolonged one, you may feel like your faith has been beaten and battered. Perhaps it feels like you are hanging on by a thread. But Jesus said, "If you have faith as a mustard seed . . . nothing will be impossible for you" (Matthew 17:20). If you didn't have a mustard seed of faith, you wouldn't be reading this right now. You would have already given up. I want to stir you up to believe God for your miracle. Believe Him *more* than you believe the doctors, medicine, the natural "facts," or what your mind and emotions tell you. God has a miracle with your name on it if you will unleash the power of your faith.

## According to Your Faith

The Gospel of Mark tells the story of a woman with a medical condition called an "issue of blood" that caused her to bleed for twelve years. She had gone to every doctor she could find and spent all her money, but no one could help her. Instead, she got worse (Mark 5:26). Not only that, but she was regarded as unclean because of her condition and treated like an outcast. On top of her medical problem, she had suffered isolation, rejection, and loneliness. I can't imagine the discouragement she must have battled. Most people would have thrown in the towel and lost hope by then, but she refused to give up. She refused to accept that this was her lot in life and kept believing that one day she would be healed. She was going to get her healing if it was the last thing she did.

When she heard Jesus was visiting her town, she ignored the cultural rules that told her to stay away and not touch anyone. She was desperate. The stories of Jesus had ignited her faith to believe this was her breakthrough moment. She said, "If only I may touch His clothes, I shall be made well" (Mark 5:28). Not, *Maybe I'll be made well*, or *I've tried everything else; I might as well try this*. No, this lady said, "If I can just get to Jesus, *I shall be healed*." Faith is not just wishing or hoping something will happen. It is being fully persuaded that God has both the power and desire to heal you. Faith is when you don't see anything happening or your situation has gotten worse, but you keep standing on the promises of God. Faith is when you don't see how it could happen, but you keep trusting God anyway.

With a determined spirit, she pushed her way through the crowd. The crowd represents everything we have to fight through to get our breakthrough: bad reports from the doctor, discouragement, fear, and other challenges. We have to press through the challenges with a tough, determined, never-say-die faith. When the lady finally got to Jesus and touched His robe, she was immediately healed. Jesus stopped and said, "Who touched Me?" (Mark 5:30). "Lord, lots of people touched You," His disciples answered (Mark 5:31). "Somebody touched Me, for *I perceived power going out from Me*" (Luke 8:46). Jesus wasn't paying attention to this woman or intentionally directing power her way, but her faith drew it out of Him and stopped Him in His tracks. Faith is what gets God's attention and draws on His miracle-working power. He pointed her out in the crowd and said, "Daughter, *your faith has made you well*" (Mark 5:34). All the people who touched Jesus that day had needs, but this lady had faith. God cares about our needs, but He responds to our faith.

**God *cares* about our needs, but He responds to our *faith*.**

Like Jesus told this woman, your faith is essential to receiving your healing. This principle is repeated in several stories in the New Testament. On one occasion, two blind men approached Jesus wanting to be healed. He asked them, "*Do you believe I am able to do this?*" He's asking you the same question today: Do you believe He is able to heal you? Do you believe Him more than you believe the doctors? More than the natural "facts"? More than your own thoughts and emotions? That is the meaning of faith. It is believing God above all else. Those two blind men had no hope in the natural of being healed, but they had heard about Jesus' miracles and were stirred in their faith to believe. Jesus said, "*According to your faith let it be to you*" and healed them both (Matthew 9:28–30). After healing another blind man named Bartimaeus, He told him, "Go your way; *your faith has made you well*" (Mark 10:52). To a Roman soldier who asked Jesus to heal his servant, He said, "*As you have believed, so let it be done for you*" (Matthew 8:13). The apostle Paul healed a man who was crippled from birth, and the Scripture says, "Paul, observing him intently and *seeing that he had faith to be healed*, said with a loud voice, 'Stand up straight on your feet!' And he leaped and walked" (Acts 14:8–10). Do you see the pattern? In every case, it was their faith that brought about the miracle. It's great to have other people praying for us, but ultimately our own faith determines what we receive from God.

Maybe you have been battling your illness for a while. Maybe you have faith fatigue. You're tired of fighting. Tired of believing. Tired of hoping. I'm asking you to dig deep, stir up your faith, and refuse to give up. Wake up every day believing this could be the day you get your miracle. The lady with the issue of blood had waited twelve long years for her healing, but she stayed in faith and refused to give up. One day, her miracle came suddenly. God doesn't move on our timetable, but when He does, He moves suddenly.

## A Lady Named Dodie

Dodie Osteen (or "Mama Dodie," as thousands affectionately call her) is the matriarch of Lakewood Church in Houston, Texas, which she and her husband started in 1959. In 1981, when she was in her forties, she was diagnosed with stage 4 metastatic liver cancer. She had several walnut-sized tumors in her liver that had spread to other parts of her body. Doctors told her she probably had six weeks to live and that chemotherapy would do little to extend her life. Faced with this life-threatening situation, she and her husband went home and prayed hard about what they should do. Given that doctors said she had little time to live with or without treatment, she felt led to forego the treatment and believe God for a miracle.

Every day, she took deliberate steps to unleash the power of her faith, but for a while it seemed to have no effect. In fact, her situation got worse. She got down to 89 pounds and was as yellow as a banana from jaundice. Many days, she was so weak she could barely get out of bed. But she kept pressing through and using her faith, even though there was nothing in the natural to encourage her.

Six weeks went by, and she was still alive. Then twelve weeks. A year went by, and Dodie never let up on her faith routine. It took a while for her to see any fruit, but eventually she was completely healed of cancer. That was forty years ago, and she is still going strong at 88 today. She has more energy than most people half her age. Her story is not only a testament to the power of faith, but a model for how to practically unleash it. Below are the steps she took to unleash her faith and receive her miracle:

**1. She kept God's Word in front of her.** Every day, she read the Word of God and used it to renew her mind and strengthen her spirit. She put healing Scriptures all over her house and used them to encourage her faith and keep her mind going in the right direction. When you are battling an illness, there is so much depleting you every day. You have to be proactive about letting God fill you back up by spending time in His Word, prayer, and worship.

**2. She spoke God's healing promises over herself multiple times a day.** This is one of the most powerful things you can do to release your faith. The Bible says God watches over His Word to perform it and it will accomplish every purpose for which He sends it (Jeremiah 1:12; Isaiah 55:11). I cover this topic extensively in the next chapter and provide you a list of Scripture confessions to speak over yourself daily.

**3. She acted like she was well.** She has said, "If I really believed I was healed, then I needed to act like it." She refused to let people treat her like a sick person. Even when she was so weak she could barely get out of bed, she made herself get up, go down to the church, and minister to others. The Scripture says, "Faith without works is dead" (James 2:20, 26). That was how she put works to her faith. Sometimes the best thing we can do when we are going through a trial is to help someone else. That helps us get our mind off our own problems and reminds us we're not the only one walking through a trial. Even if you are in bed in the hospital, try to do something to encourage everyone who walks in your door. I ministered to a lady who had cancer all over her body and went through two years of grueling treatments. She and her husband made bagged lunches every week and took them to the homeless on the streets of Houston, even though she suffered in her body daily. They were putting works to their faith and sowing a seed for their own need. The Scripture says that as we help others, God will help us (Proverbs 11:25; Galatians 6:7).

**4. She kept pictures of herself around the house from a time when she was healthier and more vibrant.** One was a picture taken on her wedding day. Another was of her sitting on a horse. These inspiring images gave her a vision of herself healthy and vibrant to attach her faith to. You have to see yourself as healthy on the inside with your eyes of faith before it will ever come to pass on the outside. God gave us an imagination so we could have faith for things we cannot see in the natural.

In Genesis 11:6, God said about people's imagination, "Nothing they have imagined . . . will be impossible for them" (AMPC). That's because when we imagine something, we attach our faith to it, and nothing is impossible with faith. The enemy knows this, too. That's why he tries to hijack our imagination by getting us to imagine the worst thing happening. Instead, every day you need to purposely imagine yourself healthy again and living a wonderful, fulfilling life.

A man at our church was involved in a terrible car wreck that shattered the bones in his hips and both of his legs. The doctors said he probably would never walk again, and he certainly would never run. He had been a track star in high school and college, so he put pictures around his house of himself running in his younger days. Every day, he imagined himself running again. He believed God for it. In just three months, he was not only walking but running again. That is the power of your imagination and faith.

**5. She wrote a letter to every family member and close friend apologizing to them for anything she had ever done to hurt or offend them.** She did not want anything that could block her from receiving her healing. Romans 12:18 says, "So far as it depends on you, be at peace with all people" (NASB). If you think there is anything between you and anyone else, do your best to make peace. You can't control their response, but you can do your part, and God will honor you for it. I will cover this more in chapter 6.

## Bulldog Faith

The people I have seen receive miraculous healings were like Mama Dodie and the woman with the issue of blood. They had what I call bulldog faith. Bulldogs were bred in England in the 1200s for the sport of bullfighting. They would latch on to a bull and hold on for dear life to avoid being thrown into the air and trampled. That's how they became famous for their iron grip and refusal to let go. If you want to receive a miracle healing from God, you have to be like that bulldog. Grab hold of God's healing promises and refuse to let go. Keep believing God no matter what the doctors say, what it looks like, or how you feel. Have a tough, tenacious, never-say-die faith. Your attitude should be, *This sickness is not going to defeat me. I don't accept this sickness. This is not how I'm going out.*

**If you are going to *win* the battle for your healing, you have to have a *fighting* spirit.**

I've seen far too many people give up too easily when they get a bad diagnosis. They act like whatever the doctor has said is the final word. They passively accept their sickness. If you are going to win the battle for your healing, you have to have a fighting spirit. It's never over until God says it's over.

My mother-in-law, Bea, was a great example of bulldog faith. It seemed like she had almost every ailment in the book: skin cancer, lung cancer, diabetes, heart disease, four aneurysms in her brain, and many other illnesses. She was also T-boned in her small car by a huge garbage truck when she was in her seventies and sustained serious injuries. She had sepsis once—a deadly blood infection that attacks all the vital organs—and almost died. Her blood pressure plunged to 59/18, and all her organs shut down.

But Bea was a fighter. She was the opposite of passive. She refused to accept her diseases as her lot in life. In fact, she didn't like talking about them or people making a fuss over her when she was in the hospital. Talking about your sickness and pain just gives them more life. Bea always had faith that her condition would improve, and it did time and time again. Just when we would think she was at the end, she would rally back. It was amazing. I nicknamed her the Unsinkable Bea Clark because nothing could keep her down. I used to joke that she had more lives than a cat because she cheated death over and over the last twenty years of her life. That's the kind of faith you have to have. Fighters win the battle.

The apostle Paul told his protégé, Timothy, to "fight the good fight of faith" (1 Timothy 6:12). Faith is a fight. The enemy is not going to roll out the red carpet and allow you to receive a miracle easily. He doesn't want you to fulfill your destiny or God to get any glory from your healing. He's going to fight you for it. For God's part, He doesn't heal everyone instantly because He wants us to develop a tough, durable faith that doesn't fold when we encounter adversity or don't get the result we hoped for right away. God is looking for faith warriors, like Bea, who won't back down from a fight.

Paul was such a fighter. He was beaten, stoned, shipwrecked three times, thrown in prison several times, and suffered many other things, but he just kept coming. In one passage, the Jews stoned Paul, dragged him out of the city, and left him for dead. Some believers came and attended to him, but instead of seeking refuge in another city, Paul got up and went right back into the city where he was stoned (Acts 14:19, 21). No adversity could stop him. He said, "The Holy Spirit testifies in every city, saying that chains and tribulations await me. But none of these things move me" (Acts 20:23–24). God never said the walk of faith would be easy. Sometimes it's a knock-down, drag-out, bare-knuckles fight. I'm asking you to have this "None of these things move me" kind of faith. Don't let anything or anyone move you off your faith. Paul called it the *good fight* of faith because God is on our side and every battle we face will end in victory if we stay in faith and don't quit.

## Whose Report Will You Believe?

When battling an illness, you are presented with all kinds of reports. There's the doctor's report—his or her findings and prognosis. Doctors do their best to care for us based on their human understanding. We respect and appreciate doctors, of course, but they are not all-knowing or all-powerful, nor do they have the final say. But so many people deify doctors and treat their report like it's gospel. This is by far the biggest reason I've seen for people relinquishing their faith.

I ministered by phone to a lady whose mother had just been diagnosed with stage 4 cancer. She said her mother had always been the most positive, faith-filled person, but the moment she got that report from the doctor, her whole demeanor changed. She immediately accepted it as a foregone conclusion and laid down her faith. She even started giving her possessions away and planning for her death.

If you are going to win the battle for your healing, you cannot believe the doctor's report over God's. Doctors and medicine are limited, but God is not. Often, when doctors and medicine reach their end, that's when God does His greatest miracles. Your attitude should be, *Come what may, I am going to believe God above all else. I am going to stand in faith until I draw my last breath.*

There is also the enemy's report. He doesn't want to see you healed, so he'll whisper in your mind, *You're never going to get over this. You might as well give up. God's not going to heal you. If He cared about you, He would have healed you by now. You don't deserve to be healed after the life you've lived.*

Then there is the report of your own mind. You may have all kinds of fears, imaginations, doubts, and "what-if's" coursing through your mind.

There is the report of other people, like your family and friends. Everybody has an opinion and a faith perspective, depending on their own walk with the Lord (or lack thereof).

Finally, and most importantly, there is God's report. God's report says that Jesus already bore your sicknesses and pains upon Himself at the cross and that by His stripes you were healed; that God heals all your diseases; that no weapon formed against you will prosper; that in all things you're more than a conqueror; and that God will satisfy you with long life.

Among all of these competing reports, you have to decide which one you are going to believe. Nobody else can make that decision for you.

When I was dating my wife, the knuckles on her hands became very red and inflamed. She also had severe pain in her knees and feet. At the time, she drove a sports car with a stick shift, and her knuckles hurt so badly she could barely shift gears. She finally went to the doctor and after a lot of testing was diagnosed with rheumatoid arthritis at the age of 22. Her grandmother had the same disease, and it twisted all her joints and crippled her.

Wanting a second opinion, my wife tried to get an appointment with one of the top rheumatoid doctors in the world. This man was so sought after, he was not accepting new patients, but he agreed to see my wife because she was so young and her case intrigued him.

After her appointment and further testing, we waited anxiously for his prognosis. Unfortunately, it was worse than we imagined. He said my wife would probably be crippled by the age of thirty and should never have children because they could be born with serious deformities.

You can imagine how devastated we were. But after the initial shock, something rose up inside us, and we decided to believe God's report instead of the report of that renowned doctor. We were young in our faith and didn't know much about healing, but we just decided to believe God.

One day, my wife's brother invited her to go to an event at his church where an evangelist known for healing would be ministering. The man prayed over her, and though her symptoms did not go away immediately, she felt something inside and believed she was healed. Over the next few weeks, the redness and pain in her joints dissipated every day until they were completely gone.

That was 28 years ago, and she's never had any problems since. We also have two beautiful, healthy daughters. I'm telling you, God is a healing God! Stretch your faith and believe for your healing.

A few years ago, I went to the hospital to pray for a girl with an inoperable tumor. The best doctors in the world were out of options, and their report was dire. They did not give her long to live. But the girl and her parents were undaunted. They chose to believe God's report that Jesus bore her cancer on Himself at the cross and by His stripes she was healed. Their faith was so inspiring.

After we talked, the four of us had a powerful time of prayer and worshiping God for about an hour. You could feel the atmosphere in the room shift as we worshiped and released our faith. The presence of God was palpable. Later, the mom told me the presence of God had stayed in the room after I left. A couple of days later, the girl had another MRI. When the doctor examined the results, he was dumbfounded. He said, "There is no way to explain this medically, but the tumor is gone." It had completely vanished!

But the story gets even better. After that girl got healed and discharged from the hospital, a toddler with a brain tumor checked in and got her same room and bed. He had already been treated at another hospital, and there was nothing more they could do, so they transferred him to this hospital as a last-ditch effort. The doctors told his parents they didn't think he would live much longer. But the power and presence of God were still lingering in that room from when we prayed for the teenage girl. Amazingly, God touched that little boy, and his tumor vanished, too!

Both miracles may have manifested suddenly, but the families had been praying in faith for over a year. They kept believing God's report even though their children's conditions got worse. Their persistent faith laid the groundwork for God finally to move suddenly.

God did not just do miracles in Bible times; He's doing them today. The Bible says He never changes. He will never stop healing people and doing miracles. If God did it for others, He can do it for you. He doesn't love them any more than He loves you.

## Feed Your Faith

There is an old saying: "You are what you eat." That truism applies not only to our body, but to our mind and spirit as well. What you feed your mind and spirit every day will determine how victorious you are in overcoming your illness. Battling a serious illness can challenge your faith like nothing else. It can deplete and wear you down physically, mentally, emotionally, and spiritually. Unfortunately, most of the patients I have visited don't seem to be doing much to counteract this. Usually, when I walk into their room, they are watching a game show, soap opera, or something similar on TV. Most Christian patients also don't have their Bibles with them in their rooms. There is virtually nothing and no one feeding their faith. You cannot win the battle that way. You have to be intentional and determined about feeding your faith and strengthening yourself spiritually every day.

Fortunately, you have more ways than ever before to feed your faith and strengthen yourself. If there are no Christian channels in your hospital room, there are YouTube videos, podcasts, and ministries that live-stream and post preaching messages online every day. You can download the YouVersion Bible app onto your phone; it has the Bible, daily devotionals, and Bible on audio. You can also listen to praise and worship music on your phone or other device.

On the flip side, I encourage you to avoid people and things that diminish your faith. These include reading online about how dire your condition is and what the survival rate is; listening to doubting, worrisome family members; obsessing over what the doctor said; and meditating on fearful thoughts. If you avoid the wrong things and feed on the right things, you will keep your faith and spirit strong and position yourself to receive your healing.

Here are some practical ways to feed your faith and strengthen yourself daily:

**Feed on God's Word every day.** Romans 10:17 says that "faith comes by hearing, and hearing by the word of God." This verse tells us plainly how faith comes—by hearing the Word of God. You can listen to faith-filled preaching in church, on Christian TV, on YouTube, online, in podcasts, or on SiriusXM radio. You can also listen to the Bible on audio or speak Scriptures aloud. There have never been more ways to hear the Word of God. The more you feed on God's Word, the more your spirit will be nourished and strengthened, and the more your faith will grow.

Reading God's Word has the same faith-building effect as hearing it audibly. The famous evangelist D. L. Moody once said,

> I prayed for faith and thought that someday faith would come down and strike me like lightning. But faith did not seem to come. One day I read in the tenth chapter of Romans, "Faith cometh by hearing, and hearing by the Word of God." I had up to this time closed my Bible and prayed for faith. I now opened my Bible and began to study, and faith has been growing ever since.[1]

As you spend time daily reading and meditating on God's Word, you will hear Him speaking to you through it—not out loud, but down in your spirit. It will also help you renew your mind and keep your thoughts going in the right direction. When battling a serious illness, all kinds of vexing thoughts will try to enter your mind. The enemy knows if he can control your thoughts and get you to operate in fear, negativity, and doubt instead of faith, he can win the battle for your healing. You can't be passive about your thought life. As you fill your mind with God's Word, there won't be room for defeated thoughts, and you will program your mind for victory.

**Keep things in front of you that encourage your faith.** It is so important that you surround yourself with things that encourage and inspire you and strengthen your faith. Don't allow your home or hospital room to become dreary and depressing. You need to create an environment that fosters your faith, lifts your spirit, and invites the presence of God. Like Mama Dodie, put healing and other inspirational Scriptures all around your hospital room or house. Keep pictures around of when you were healthy, vibrant, and enjoying life. Imagine yourself like that again and attach your faith to those images. You have to see it on the inside with your eyes of faith before it will ever happen on the outside. See yourself totally healed and living a long, satisfying life.

**You have to see it on the *inside* with your eyes of faith before it will ever happen on the *outside*.**

**Listen to faith-building testimonies.** Hearing testimonies of what God has done in other people's lives builds our own faith. That's why I put a lot of healing testimonies in this book. Christian TV is also a great source of encouraging testimonies. Two of my favorite shows that have great testimonies are the *700 Club* on CBN and Sid Roth's *It's Supernatural*. If you don't have Christian channels on your TV, you can watch both shows online. When you hear a great testimony, write it down in a journal and keep a collection of them. Read over them often to remind yourself that God is a miracle-working God and nothing is impossible with Him. God is no respecter of persons. What He did for someone else, He can do for you if you have the faith to receive it.

**Remember what God has done in your life.** Think about all the trials God has brought you through over the years, the miracles He has done in your life, the things He has protected and delivered you from, and the ways He has come through for you when it looked hopeless. If God did it before, He will do it again! As you stay in faith during your healing process, you are going to see God do amazing things in your life, both small and large. You're also going to experience Him in ways you never have before. I have heard this countless times from people battling illness. I encourage you to keep a journal of all the answered prayers, the victories, and the special people God brings to help you along the way. Over time, we tend to forget all that He has done for us. From time to time, read through this journal to remind yourself of all the things God has done in your life and how faithful He's been. This will strengthen your faith.

### *Prayer for Faith*

*Father God, thank You that Jesus said if I have a mustard seed of faith, nothing will be impossible. Help me to have the faith I need to receive my healing. Help me to believe You more than I believe the doctors and medicine, the natural facts, or my own thoughts and emotions. When I feel weak in my faith, I ask You to revive, refresh, and strengthen it. Help me to have tough, determined, never-say-die faith. Guard my heart and mind from fear, worry, doubt, lies, and anything else that would undermine my faith. Help me to take steps every day to feed my faith and unleash its power. God, I confess that You have all power and are well able to heal me. I believe You for my complete healing, wholeness, and restoration. In Jesus' mighty name, Amen.*

## UNLOCKING HEALING WITH KEY 2: *Healing Scriptures*

How to use these Scriptures:

1. Put them up around your house or hospital room. Read them several times a day. Meditate on them. Memorize them. They will strengthen your faith and help you maintain a victorious mindset.
2. Speak them over yourself. Personalize them and make them your own. They belong to you. As we just discussed about the power of faith, believe that you have the title deed to them, accept them as fact, and keep believing them, no matter what.
3. Incorporate them into your prayers. God is not bound by anything but His Word, and He likes to hear His Word quoted back to Him. For example, you can say in your prayers, "God, You said Jesus bore all my sicknesses and infirmities upon Himself at the cross and that by His stripes I am healed. Thank You that Jesus already paid the price for my healing. I receive complete healing, wholeness, and restoration in every part of my body right now, in Jesus' name."

"For I am the LORD who heals you" (Exodus 15:26).

"I will take sickness away from the midst of you" (Exodus 23:25).

"I have heard your prayer, I have seen your tears; surely I will heal you" (2 Kings 20:5).

"For I will restore health to you and heal you of your wounds" (Jeremiah 30:17).

"Bless the LORD, O my soul, and forget not all His benefits: who forgives all your iniquities, who heals all your diseases" (Psalm 103:2–3).

"However, it was our sicknesses that He Himself bore, and our pains that He carried. . . . And by his wounds we are healed"[2] (Isaiah 53:4–5 NASB).

"He Himself [Jesus] took our infirmities and bore our sicknesses" (Matthew 8:17).

"By his wounds you have been healed" (1 Peter 2:24 NIV).

"Beloved, I wish above all things that thou mayest prosper and be in health, even as thy soul prospereth" (3 John 1:2 KJV).

"O LORD my God, I cried out to You, and You healed me" (Psalm 30:2).

"You restore my health and allow me to live" (Isaiah 38:16 NLT).

"Heal me, O LORD, and I shall be healed" (Jeremiah 17:14).

"[God's] word [is] health to all their flesh" (Proverbs 4:20–22).

"You will live a long life and see my saving power" (Psalm 91:16 CEV).

"I shall not die, but live, and declare the works of the LORD" (Psalm 118:17).

"[God] performs wonders that cannot be fathomed, miracles that cannot be counted" (Job 5:9 NIV).

"Behold, I am the LORD, the God of all flesh. Is there anything too hard for Me?" (Jeremiah 32:27).

"Lord GOD! It is you who have made the heavens and the earth by your great power and by your outstretched arm! Nothing is too hard for you" (Jeremiah 32:17 ESV).

"All things are possible with God" (Mark 10:27 AMP).

"What is impossible with men is possible with God" (Luke 18:27 AMPC).

"If you can believe, all things are possible to him who believes" (Mark 9:23).

"If you have faith as a mustard seed . . . nothing will be impossible for you" (Matthew 17:20).

"No weapon formed against you shall prosper" (Isaiah 54:17).

"The righteous cry out, and the LORD hears, and delivers them out of all their troubles" (Psalm 34:17).

"God is our refuge and strength, a very present help in trouble" (Psalm 46:1).

"I will never fail you. I will never abandon you" (Hebrews 13:5 NLT).

"So Abraham prayed to God; and God healed Abimelech, his wife, and his female servants" (Genesis 20:17).

"Then they cried out to the LORD in their trouble, and He saved them out of their distresses. He sent His word and healed them, and delivered them from their destructions. Oh, that men would give thanks to the LORD for His goodness, and for His wonderful works to the children of men!" (Psalm 107:19–21).

"Is anyone among you sick? Let him call for the elders of the church, and let them pray over him, anointing him with oil in the name of the Lord. And the prayer of faith will save the sick, and the Lord will raise him up" (James 5:14–15).

KEY 3

# Miracle in Your Mouth

> Death and life are in the power of the tongue.
>
> Proverbs 18:21

> Words are containers for power.
>
> Joyce Meyer

IN THE LAST CHAPTER, we explored how faith is the currency of heaven and essential for receiving healing or anything else from God. Faith is not just something we have inside. It is not enough just to believe inside or think faith-filled thoughts. Faith is like salt in a saltshaker. Salt does no one any good sitting in the shaker. It must be released onto our food to have any effect. In the same way, faith must be released from inside of us to have any effect. One of the most important ways we do this is through *our words*. Faith-filled words spoken out of your mouth are one of the most powerful tools in your arsenal for healing. Your own mouth may hold the key to your miracle if you learn to harness its power.

## The Power of Words

The Bible has much to say about the power of our words. Proverbs 18:21 says, "Death and life are in the power of the tongue, and those who love it will eat its fruit." Just understanding and applying this one verse can radically change your life. It says that our tongue holds the power of life and death. Is there any greater power than the power of life and death? God says He put that power in our own mouths. That means we have the power to speak life or death over ourselves, our situation, and our loved ones. When we are battling a serious illness, or caring for a loved one who is, our words can greatly influence the outcome. People can hinder their own or a loved one's healing without even realizing it because of their words. You can pray the most powerful prayers in the world and then cancel those prayers by speaking words of doubt, defeat, and negativity. If you want to experience healing and victory, you must train your mouth and wield its power carefully. Life and death are in the power of the tongue!

The second part of this verse says you will eat the fruit of your words. Your words are producing fruit in your life. They can produce good fruit or bad fruit. The power of the tongue cuts both ways. You have to speak words that will produce the kind of fruit you want. That means speaking faith, victory, and God's healing promises every day. It also means avoiding speaking doubt, fear, and negativity, or repeating negative reports from the doctor over and over. If you have a negative, defeated mouth, you are going to have a negative, defeated life. You can't talk sickness and have health. You can't talk defeat and have victory. Your words are producing fruit. You are calling in whatever you speak out of your mouth. I'm asking you to call in healing, call in life, call in victory.

I know someone who is always talking about what is wrong in his body and the problems in his life. Every time someone tries to encourage him, he says, "But the problem is . . ." He would rather talk about the problem than speak faith and victory. Consequently, for all the years I have known him, he has had one sickness and crisis after another. Your life is going to follow your words. When you change what you are saying, you will change what you are seeing.

**When you change what you are *saying*, you will change what you are *seeing*.**

One time, Jesus was hungry and saw a fig tree from a distance. He hoped the tree had figs on it, but when He got close, He saw there were none. Disappointed, Jesus spoke to the tree and said, "May no one ever eat fruit from you again" (Mark 11:14 NIV).

Jesus' disciples had seen His words have an immediate effect before. When they were in a boat on the Sea of Galilee and got caught in a storm, He commanded the winds and waves to stop, and they immediately obeyed Him (Mark 4:39). When He said, "Lazarus, come forth!" Lazarus was instantly raised from the dead (John 11:43). But this time, it seemed like His words had no effect on the tree. It looked exactly the same on the outside. But on the inside, the tree was already dead because of Jesus' words. When you speak to your sickness or your situation, you may not see instant results. But make no mistake: Your words have power, and their effect will manifest in time. The next day, Jesus' disciples were astonished when they saw the fig tree and said, "Rabbi, look! The fig tree you cursed has withered!" (Mark

11:21 NIV). The word *cursed* doesn't mean Jesus used profanity; it means He spoke negatively to it. Jesus' explanation to His disciples is one of the greatest passages in the Bible on the power of words. He said:

> Have faith in God. For assuredly, I say to you, whoever *says* to this mountain, "Be removed and be cast into the sea," and does not doubt in his heart, but believes that those things he *says* will be done, *he will have whatever he says.*
>
> Mark 11:22–23

Notice Jesus didn't say, "The tree died because I am God, and that's how powerful My words are." He talked about the power of *our* words. He said when we have faith, our words can move mountains. Your "mountain" is your sickness or whatever is standing between you and what God promised you. You have the power to speak directly to that sickness or disease and command it to be removed from your body in Jesus' name.

Jesus said "whoever says *to this mountain*," not "whoever says to God about this mountain." Don't just tell God about your mountain (He already knows). Tell the mountain about your God. Tell the mountain how big and powerful your God is and that it is no match for your God.

Jesus also did not tell us to complain about the mountain or tell all our friends about the mountain. He did not even tell us to pray about the mountain, even though prayer is certainly important and powerful. He told us to *speak to the mountain*. Every day, you need to speak to your sickness and say, "Cancer, heart disease, diabetes (or whatever), I command you to go from my body, in Jesus' name. I command every cell in my body to line up with the Word of God, which says I am healed by the stripes of Jesus. I command healing, wholeness, and restoration to every part of my body, in the mighty name of Jesus." When you do this, make sure you speak with faith and authority.

A while back, a heavy object in our garage fell on my wife's head, and she sustained a severe concussion. When I took her to the emergency room, she could not tell the doctor who the president was or what year it was. She had severe cognitive and memory issues, headaches, and trouble speaking for over a week. We prayed for her healing every day but saw very little progress. She is a Realtor, and about ten days after her concussion, she had a closing. She woke up the morning of her closing with a bad headache and difficulty speaking. During our morning prayer time, we felt prompted to speak to the concussion and command healing, according to the passage above. Over the next hour, I spoke healing over her. We still didn't see any progress. Finally, in faith she got in the car and started driving to her closing. With great difficulty forming her words, she kept speaking healing over herself. She spoke to her brain and commanded it to function perfectly, commanded headaches to go, and commanded her speech to be normal. By the time she got to her closing, she was totally healed. I was with her for the rest of the day, and she had no more symptoms whatsoever. When we do what Jesus instructed us to do and speak to our mountains with faith, miracles happen. There is a miracle in your mouth!

Besides commanding sicknesses and symptoms to leave our bodies, there is another powerful application of the passages above. Just like Jesus "cursed" the fig tree and it withered and died, we can "curse" or speak death over cancer cells, tumors, diseases, and sickness. Remember Proverbs 18:21? "Death and life are in the power of the tongue." Jesus did not make the fig tree wither and die just for kicks. He was teaching us a lesson and setting an example about the power of our words. If you are battling cancer, for example, you can say, "As Jesus cursed the fig tree and it withered and died, I curse all cancer cells in my body at the root and command them to wither and die and bear no more fruit, in Jesus' mighty name." You can apply this verbiage to whatever your sickness or disease is.

Usually, this doesn't work like a magic wand where you say it once and *presto!* everything is perfect again. Even when Jesus cursed the fig tree, it did not wither and die right away. Those words manifested slowly overnight. Most of the time, it takes time for the effect of your words to manifest. It may take weeks or months to see the result. You have to be *persistent*. But if you keep using your words in the right way, one day your breakthrough will come suddenly.

The people I have seen receive miraculous healings used their words to speak faith and victory. They didn't rehearse the problem and how bad they felt. They didn't obsess over the negative doctor's report. Instead, they focused on God's report and declared what His Word said about their situation. You may feel like complaining or talking about your sickness and how bad you feel, but that's going to keep you stuck where you are. Don't use your words to describe your situation; use your words to change your situation. Joel 3:10 says, "Let the weak say, 'I am strong.'" It doesn't say let the weak say they are weak. Don't speak the problem; speak what you want. Phrase things in a way that puts faith into the atmosphere. Instead of repeating what the doctor said over and over as if it is gospel, say, "The doctor gave a different report, but God's report says

**Don't use your words to *describe* your situation; use your words to *change* your situation.**

I am healed by the stripes of Jesus." Instead of saying, "I don't know if I'll ever get well," say, "God is healing me day by day. I'm getting healthier and stronger. My best days are ahead of me."

This isn't denying the natural facts or being hyper-spiritual. It is recognizing that there is a truth and a power that supersedes the natural facts. The natural facts are not the end of the story, and the doctors don't have the final say. God does. His power is greater than doctors, medicine, and the natural facts. He is a miracle-working God.

Galatians 3:5 says, "Therefore He who supplies the Spirit to you and works miracles among you, does He do it by the works of the law, or *by the hearing of faith*?" It is by the hearing of faith that God works miracles. God needs to hear faith coming out of your mouth. Before being healed by Jesus, the woman with the issue of blood said to herself, "If only I may touch His clothes, I shall be made well." The two blind men Jesus healed said, "Lord, we believe you can heal us" (Matthew 9:28). The Roman soldier whose servant Jesus healed said, "Just speak a word and my servant will be healed" (Matthew 8:8). The leper who was healed said, "You can make me clean" (Mark 1:40–42). In each case, they verbalized their faith and released it into the atmosphere through their words. Then their healing came.

In Ezekiel 37, the prophet had a vision where he was standing in the middle of a valley full of dead, dry bones. God asked Ezekiel an interesting question: "Son of man, can these bones live?" (Ezekiel 37:3). Most of us would have answered, "Of course not. These dead, dry bones can't live." But Ezekiel gave a careful answer: "O Lord God, You know" (Ezekiel 37:3). Then God told Ezekiel to prophesy (speak) to those bones and command them to come to life. When Ezekiel did, the bones started to rattle. Ligaments formed and connected the bones together. Muscles and tendons began to grow over the bones, and then skin covered them. But these newly formed bodies were still dead. So God told Ezekiel to speak to them again and command them to come to life. When he did, breath suddenly entered them, and a vast army came to life.

The purpose of this dramatic vision was to teach Ezekiel—and us—about the power of our words. It looked like Ezekiel was in a hopeless situation—a valley full of useless, dead bones. It looked like nothing good could come out of that situation. But when Ezekiel began to use his words to command them to come to life, those old bones turned into a living army! In the same way, God wants you to use your words to change your situation. Prophesy to the dead, dry bones in your life. Speak life, healing, victory. Speak to your body like Ezekiel spoke to those bones and say, "Body, I command you to line up with the Word of God, which says I am healed by the stripes of Jesus. I declare my body is healthy, strong, and full of energy." You are not limited by your sickness or circumstances; you are limited by your words. Speak healing, and healing will come. Speak victory, and victory will come. Your life will follow your words.

## Faith Cocoon

The Scripture says Jesus did not do many mighty works in His hometown because of the people's unbelief (Matthew 13:58). God does not operate the way He wants to in an atmosphere of unbelief. You can't afford to take chances with people being careless with their words and speaking death over you or your loved one or having an attitude of unbelief. Because of what the Bible teaches about the power of words, I encourage people who are battling a serious illness to create a "faith cocoon." That means you quarantine yourself or your loved one from anyone who would bring doubt, fear, or negativity into the atmosphere. You need to create an atmosphere of faith that invites the presence of God and His miracle-working power. Don't allow family members and friends to speak any doubt or negativity in your presence. Make it known that only words of faith will be spoken in your room.

If the doctor has some negative news to share and your loved one is semiconscious or unconscious, it is best to talk to the doctor outside the room. Patients who are unconscious can still hear everything that is said. Having a doctor or loved one speak death over them can discourage them and dampen their faith. So be careful about what is spoken around them. This is not about being in denial or being super-spiritual. It is about recognizing the power of words and the importance of maintaining faith, and taking commonsense steps to guard against words of doubt and death.

One time, a man named Jairus asked Jesus if He would visit his house and heal his daughter, who was near death. Before Jesus could get there, word came that the girl had died. Jesus told Jairus, "Do not be afraid; only believe" (Mark 5:36). He knew He needed faith present to perform a miracle, so He only allowed Peter, James, and John, His closest disciples, to go with Him. When they arrived at the home, people were weeping and wailing loudly. Jesus said to them, "Why make this commotion and weep? The child is not dead, but sleeping" (Mark 5:39). The people in the house ridiculed Jesus for saying that. So guess what He did? *He put them all outside* (Mark 5:40). He knew their unbelief would hinder His ability to do a miracle. That was Jesus making a faith cocoon. Once the critics and naysayers were out, Jesus told the girl to arise, and she immediately came back to life.

Peter, following Jesus' example, did the same thing when he went to the home of a girl who had died. There was a lot of weeping and commotion in the home. Knowing the people had already accepted the girl's death as fact and would not have faith to believe for a miracle, "*Peter put them all out*, and knelt down and prayed" (Acts 9:40). Peter had to create a faith cocoon so the power of God could move. Then he looked at the girl and said, "Tabitha, arise." The girl immediately opened her eyes and sat up (Acts 9:40). These stories with Jesus and Peter are biblical precedence for protecting yourself or your loved one from doubters and naysayers. Do whatever you have to do to create an environment of faith and get your miracle.

This is what we had to do with my mother-in-law when she contracted sepsis, a life-threatening blood infection, in the hospital years ago. All her vital organs shut down. She had to be put on a ventilator and dialysis. Her blood pressure plummeted to near-fatal levels. The lead doctor told us that because of her age, she probably wouldn't make it, and even if she did, she would be in rehab for at least six months. A couple of family members started speaking doubt and even planning her funeral in the room. My wife and I had seen many miraculous healings by this point, and we were believing for another. We also knew the importance of staying in faith and the power of words. We could not allow people to speak doubt and death in my mother-in-law's room.

So my wife pulled these family members aside and told them firmly but lovingly that we couldn't have any negative words spoken in the room. She asked them only to speak faith and life. We were making a faith cocoon around her mother and protecting her from words of doubt and death that could have blocked her healing. We also put Post-it Notes all over her mom's bed with Scriptures about healing and the power of God. We prayed over her and spoke healing Scriptures over her relentlessly, did spiritual warfare (which I'll cover more in chapter 7), put praise music on in her room, and worshiped God. We did everything we could to create the right atmosphere for a miracle.

After a few days, her condition miraculously turned around, and within three weeks from the onset of sepsis, she walked out of the hospital with no need for rehab. The doctor said, "She is my miracle patient."

Here are some tips to create your own faith cocoon:

- Lovingly ask any family and friends who speak doubt, fear, or death to refrain from doing so. You may have to limit contact or even ban anyone who persists in speaking doubt or who has an attitude of unbelief.
- If your loved one is semiconscious or unconscious and the doctor has any negative news to share, ask if you can speak to them outside the room.
- Put up faith-building Scriptures around the room.
- Play praise and worship music.
- Spend time every day praying, praising God, and doing spiritual warfare. I will talk more about these in later chapters.
- Put pictures around the room of yourself or your loved one when you/they were healthy, vibrant, and enjoying life. This will give you/them a vision of health and victory to which you/they can attach your/their faith.

## Declare God's Word over Yourself

So far, I have covered what the Bible teaches about the power of our words. Now I want to pivot and focus on the power of speaking God's Word over yourself or your loved one. In chapter 2, I shared Dodie Osteen's testimony of being miraculously healed of stage 4 liver cancer. One of the main things she did was declare God's healing promises over herself relentlessly every day. The Word of God is one of the most powerful forces in the universe. Hebrews 11:3 says, "By faith we understand that the worlds were framed by the word of God." God simply said, "Let there be," and the whole universe came into existence out of nothing (Genesis 1–3). That is how incomprehensibly big and powerful God is. When He speaks, unimaginable power and miracles are released! His written Word has the same power.

In 2 Timothy 3:16 (NIV) we are told, "All Scripture is God-breathed." God's written Word contains His breath of life and supernatural power. When you speak His Word over your body, your life, and your situation, it is like God is breathing on you, and you are releasing wonder-working power into the atmosphere. Jesus said, "The words that I speak to you are *spirit* and they are *life*" (John 6:63). Hebrews 4:12 (AMP) says, "The word of God is *living* and *active* and *full of power*." These verses tell us that God's Word is *alive*. The Bible is the only book that can claim that. No other written words contain the very breath and power of Almighty God. God's Word is also *active*. When we speak it into the atmosphere, it goes to work accomplishing the purpose for which it was sent. God said His Word will not return to Him void or without having any effect, but it will accomplish every purpose for which He sent it (Isaiah 55:10–11). Jesus said not one jot or tittle of God's Word will fail to accomplish its purpose (Matthew 5:18).

The only purpose of God's healing promises is to bring healing. So when you speak His healing promises over yourself—and I encourage you to do so several times a day—

they will accomplish their purpose. God also said, "I am watching over My word to perform it" (Jeremiah 1:12 NASB). Every time you speak one of His promises over yourself or your loved one, the God of the universe is ready to perform it. I've said it before, but it bears repeating: Doing what God tells you to do doesn't always work immediately like a magic wand. You have to be persistent about making these declarations.

One time, I visited an older lady who was receiving cancer treatment. She was in from out of town and had no family or friends there to support her. She shared that she was really struggling with fear. I encouraged and prayed with her for a while, and by the time I left, she felt a lot better. I continued to visit her every week and taught her about declaring God's Word over herself daily. She didn't know anything about it, so she took notes on what I told her and wrote down every Scripture I gave her to declare over herself—verses like "God has not given [me] a spirit of fear, but of power and of love and of a sound mind" (2 Timothy 1:7); "No weapon formed against [me] shall prosper" (Isaiah 54:17); "I am healed by the stripes of Jesus" (see 1 Peter 2:24); "[God] heals all [my] diseases" (Psalm 103:3); and "With long life God will satisfy me and show me His salvation" (Psalm 91:16). Several times a day, she confessed those Scriptures over herself.

The doctors had told her she had a very low chance of survival, but to their amazement she began to make significant improvement. I encouraged her not to let up, but to keep declaring God's Word over herself many times a day. Week after week, I watched with my own eyes as this woman went from being given a virtual death sentence to being totally healed with no trace of cancer in her body. God is a healing God, and His Word brings healing to our bodies.

People often take prescription drugs several times a day and put a lot of faith in them. I'm encouraging you to take the Word of God like it is your medicine by declaring it over yourself several times a day. If you can have faith in man-made medicines and be sure to take them during the day, you can have *more* faith in the Word of Almighty God.

God said, "He who has My word, let him speak My word faithfully. Is not My word like a fire . . . and like a hammer that breaks the rock in pieces?" (Jeremiah 23:28–29). God said His Word is like a fire that can consume sickness, disease, cancer, and infection. It's like a hammer that breaks tumors, blockages, and aneurysms into pieces. But we have to do the first part of the verse: Speak His Word faithfully.

**When you *declare* God's Word over yourself, you are agreeing with it and giving it *permission* to come to pass.**

On the next page is a list of scriptural confessions to declare over yourself covering healing and other topics. Try to speak as many as you can over yourself several times a day until you have them memorized and they roll off your tongue like second nature. Personalize them and make them your own. The promises of God belong to you. *When you declare God's Word over yourself, you are agreeing with it and giving it permission to come to pass.* When you make these declarations several times a day, they will get down in your spirit, and you will start believing them. Your faith will rise, and you will live with expectancy about receiving the promises of God. They will also renew your mind so you are able to resist negative thoughts, fear, doubt, and discouragement. Remember: There is a miracle in your mouth!

## UNLOCKING HEALING WITH KEY 3: Daily Scripture Declarations

### *Healing*

- Jesus bore my sicknesses and pains upon Himself at the cross, and by His stripes I am healed (Matthew 8:17; 1 Peter 2:24).
- Jesus paid the price for my healing, and I receive it right now by faith.
- God heals all my diseases (Psalm 103:2–3).
- God has heard my prayer and seen my tears; surely He will heal me (2 Kings 20:5).
- God will restore health to me and heal all my wounds (Jeremiah 30:17).
- God is the God who heals me. He will take sickness from my midst (Exodus 15:26; 23:25).
- The healing power of God is flowing through my body. The healing power of God permeates every cell in my body. Every cell, gland, organ, and organ system is healthy, is strong, and functions the way God designed it to function. My blood, bone marrow, and immune system are healthy, strong, and function the way God designed them to function.
- The same Spirit who raised Jesus from the dead dwells in me and gives life, strength, energy, vim, vigor, and vitality to my mortal body (Romans 8:11).
- My body is the temple of the Holy Spirit, and no sickness, disease, infection, tumor, or anything that is not of God can dwell in my body (1 Corinthians 6:19).
- Jesus said in Mark 11:23 that I could command a mountain to be removed, and if I don't doubt in my

heart, I can have whatever things I say. So in the name of Jesus I command every sickness, disease, pain, and symptom to be removed from my body. I command healing, wholeness, and restoration to every cell in my body, in Jesus' mighty name.

- Because I fear the Lord and depart from evil, I am healthy and full of strength (Proverbs 3:7–8).
- With long life God will satisfy me and show me His deliverance. (Psalm 91:16).
- I will not die but live to declare the works of the Lord (Psalm 118:17).
- No weapon formed against me shall prosper (Isaiah 54:17).

### *Victory*

- I am a victor and never a victim (2 Corinthians 2:14).
- In all things, I am more than a conqueror (Romans 8:37).
- God always causes me to triumph in Christ Jesus (2 Corinthians 2:14).
- God is perfecting everything that concerns me (Psalm 138:8).
- God wishes above all things that I prosper and be in good health, even as my soul prospers. So I declare that I will be in good health and prosper in every area of my life, even as my soul prospers (3 John 1:2).
- God's goodness and mercy follow me all the days of my life (Psalm 23:6).
- God knows the plans He has for me—plans to prosper me, to give me a hope and a future (Jeremiah 29:11).

### God's Love

- God loves me passionately and calls me His child (1 John 3:1).
- God loved me even when I was a sinner and loved me before I ever loved Him, so His love is not based on my performance. I don't have to earn or deserve God's love. His love for me is unconditional and unlimited (Romans 5:8; 1 John 4:19).
- Nothing can separate me from the love of God (Romans 8:38–39).
- God will never leave nor forsake me (Hebrews 13:5).

### God's Deliverance and Protection

- God is my refuge and strength, a very present help in the time of trouble (Psalm 46:1).
- God delivers me out of all my troubles (Psalm 34:17, 19).
- God is my hiding place. He protects me from trouble and surrounds me with songs of deliverance (Psalm 32:7).
- The Lord is my rock, my fortress, and my deliverer (2 Samuel 22:2).
- God has me in the palm of His hand (Isaiah 41:10).
- God gives His angels charge over me to keep me in all my ways and bear me up in their hands (Psalm 91:11–12).

### Strength

- I can do all things through Christ, who strengthens me (Philippians 4:13).
- I am strong in the Lord and the power of His might (Ephesians 6:10).

- God has armed me with strength for the battle. He has subdued my enemies under my feet (Psalm 18:39 NLT).

### *Fear*

- God has not given me a spirit of fear, but of power, love, and a sound mind (2 Timothy 1:7).
- Fear is not from God, and I reject fear in all its forms (2 Timothy 1:7).
- I receive God's perfect love for me and let it wash over me. His perfect love casts out all fear from me (1 John 4:18).
- God is my refuge and strength, a very present help in the time of trouble. Therefore, I will not fear (Psalm 46:1–2).
- I will not be shaken or fear any negative news. My heart is steadfast, trusting in God (Psalm 112:6–7 NIV).

### *Peace*

- I am anxious for nothing, but in everything by prayer and supplication, with thanksgiving, I make my requests known to God. And the peace of God, which surpasses all understanding, will guard my heart and mind through Christ Jesus (Philippians 4:6–7).
- God keeps me in perfect peace because my mind is stayed on Him and I trust Him (Isaiah 26:3–4).
- Jesus has given me His peace, not as the world gives, but as He gives. I will not let my heart be troubled or be afraid (John 14:27).
- Peace is a fruit of the Holy Spirit who lives inside of me. I walk in the fruit of peace at all times, regardless of my circumstances (Galatians 5:22).

- The Lord blesses and keeps me and makes His face shine upon me. He is gracious to me, looks upon me with favor, and gives me peace (Numbers 6:24–26).

### *Sleep*

- When I lie down, I will not be afraid, and my sleep will be sweet (Proverbs 3:24).
- I will lie down and sleep in peace (Psalm 4:8).

### *Finances*

- God will supply all my need according to His riches in glory by Christ Jesus (Philippians 4:19).
- The Lord is my Shepherd; I shall not lack (Psalm 23:1 AMPC).
- God takes pleasure in my prosperity (Psalm 35:27). He has plans to prosper me, to give me a hope and a future (Jeremiah 29:11). God wishes above all things that I prosper (3 John 2).

KEY 4

# Prayer That Works

The prayer of faith will save the sick.

James 5:15

God does nothing except in response to believing prayer.

John Wesley

IMAGINE HAVING A PHONE that connects you straight to God. Your Healer. The One who can meet every need you have and has the solution to every problem you face. You could use the phone anytime you want, 24/7, to talk to God, present your requests to Him, and receive life-changing wisdom and guidance from Him. God would always take your call. You would never get a busy signal or His voice mail. Minus the phone, that is exactly what we have with prayer. Prayer connects us with God more than anything else. It is our lifeblood as believers, our pipeline to everything God has for us. Prayer is also one of the most powerful arrows in our quiver, a secret weapon that can turn any situation around. Psalm 56:9 (TPT, TLB) says that the very moment we pray, the tide of the battle turns. Prayer moves the hands that rule the world. It allows God to invade our situation and bring miracles. Prayer is not our last resort after we've tried everything else; it is our first and best resort. That is why the apostle Paul told us to "pray without ceasing" and to "pray about everything" (1 Thessalonians 5:17; Philippians 4:6 NLT). And that is why the enemy tries everything he can to distract, discourage, and disrupt our prayers.

Every believer has equal access to God through prayer. God doesn't have favorites. The Bible says every believer has boldness and confidence to enter His presence because of the shed blood of Jesus (Hebrews 10:19–22). We all have equal access, but not all prayers are equal. Some prayers are effective, and some are not. James 5:16 says, "The effective, fervent prayer of a righteous man avails much." Notice it is "effective" prayers that avail much. The word *effective* means there is also ineffective prayer. One time, Jesus' disciples approached Him while He was praying and said, "Lord, teach us to pray" (Luke 11:1). This request alone tells us there is an effective and an ineffective way to pray. If the disciples were already praying effectively and getting results, they wouldn't have needed to ask Jesus how to pray.

Many Christians pray ineffective prayers because they pray according to their religious tradition or their own mind instead of how the Bible teaches us to pray. In this chapter, I want to teach you how to pray effective prayers that will get results and usher in your healing.

## The Prayer of Faith

The first requirement for effective prayer is to have real faith in God and His promises. James 5:15 says, "The prayer of faith will save the sick, and the Lord will raise him up." Notice it is the prayer of *faith* that will save the sick. Not rote religious prayers. Not begging or complaining prayers. It is faith that moves God. Faith is the currency of heaven. Praying without faith is like going shopping without money. James 1:7 says without faith we cannot expect to receive anything from God. When we pray, we must believe God for what we are asking for. God is not moved by an abundance of words. He is not impressed by religiosity or flowery eloquence. What moves God is simple prayers from the heart prayed with faith.

Prayer is not talking at God, giving Him our laundry list of complaints and grievances. Prayer is not about begging God or trying to strong-arm Him into doing something. The truth is, He's already done everything He's going to do. As we talked about in chapter 1, Jesus already bore your sicknesses upon Himself at the cross and paid the price for your healing.

*Praying* **without faith is like going** *shopping* **without money.**

Martin Luther said, "Prayer is not overcoming God's reluctance, but laying hold of His willingness."[1] We lay hold of His willingness by coming into agreement with what He has already done and with His will. Through this agreement, we give it permission to manifest in our life. In Mark 11:24, Jesus said, "Whatever things you ask when you pray, believe that you *have received* it [past tense], and it *will be* yours [future tense]." You have to believe in faith that you have *already received* your healing when Jesus paid for it on the cross two thousand years ago and see yourself healed with your eyes of faith. Your mindset should be, "I am not trying to get God to heal me. I agree with God's Word that Jesus already took my infirmities on Himself at the cross and paid the price for my healing, and

I receive my healing by faith. My healing is signed, sealed, and delivered by the blood of Jesus, and I'm just waiting for it to manifest in the natural."

Recently, I went to pray for a woman who was near death in the transplant unit of one of our top hospitals. She had severe cirrhosis of the liver from alcoholism and desperately needed a transplant. The problem was, she had other serious medical issues and could not receive a new liver until those issues were resolved. Her 110-pound frame had swollen to 240 pounds because her kidneys were not functioning, and she had severe edema. The other problem was, it can take as long as a year to receive a matching liver because there are so many people on the waiting list, and she needed one right away. She needed a miracle. But I have learned not to be daunted by how bad someone looks or how dire their prognosis is. Scripture says, "We walk by faith, not by sight" (2 Corinthians 5:7). We don't go by what we see or hear in the natural. Faith is about believing what we cannot see. God is a supernatural God, and He's not limited by any natural facts or circumstances. He is only limited by lack of faith.

This lady's sister, who was a strong believer, and I joined our faith and went to war for her in the spirit realm. For over an hour, we prayed faith-filled prayers, declared God's healing promises over her, pleaded the blood of Jesus over her, did spiritual warfare, and praised God by faith for the victory. When I pray for people, I put Mark 11:24 (quoted above) to work. I believe Jesus paid the price for their healing and that their healing will come. I imagine them being totally healed and restored. I haven't always gotten the results I hoped for, but I could write an encyclopedia on all the miracles I have seen. That's why I am so passionate about it.

The next day I returned, and her edema had gone down incredibly, but she had a new problem: Her blood was not coagulating properly, and she was bleeding from every orifice in her body. So her sister and I went to war again—praying, declaring, doing spiritual warfare, and praising for another hour. The next day, her bleeding miraculously stopped. On the third day, God did another miracle, and a liver that was a perfect match suddenly became available. Today she is perfectly healthy, vibrant, and living a full life. The prayer of faith will save the sick, and the Lord will raise them up! Keep praying! Keep believing! Don't ever give up, no matter what it looks like.

### Pray the Word

The second requirement for effective prayer is that it must be according to God's will. First John 5:14–15 says, "Now this is the confidence that we have in Him, that *if we ask anything according to His will*, He hears us. And if we know that He hears us, whatever we ask, we know that we have the petitions that we have asked of Him." This verse says we can have absolute confidence when we pray according to God's will that He not only hears us, but that He will grant our petitions.

How do we know we are praying according to God's will? By praying His Word. His written Word spells out His will. God's Word is His covenant with us, and He is not bound by anything else but His Word. I have provided everything in this book to help you pray the Word. There are prayers after this chapter and throughout the book based on God's Word and a list of Scriptures after chapter 3 that you can incorporate into your prayers.

**God's Word is His *covenant* with us, and He is not bound by anything else but His *Word*.**

In Isaiah 43:26, God said, "Put Me in remembrance." He didn't say this because He has a bad memory. He likes to be reminded of His Word and have it quoted back to Him. In Jeremiah 1:12 (NASB), He said, "I am watching over My word to perform it." He's not watching over our word to perform it. He's not watching over a rote religious prayer to perform it. He is watching over His own Word to perform it. So whatever you are praying for, find some Scriptures that pertain to your request and include them in your prayer.

If you listened to me pray, you would hear me quoting many Scriptures I have memorized. You would hear me say a lot, "Father, You said . . ." or "Father, Your Word says . . ." Mainly, I remind God of what He promised. His own words will move Him more than my words will.

Let's do a quick review from chapter 1 of some healing promises from God's Word you can remind Him of in your prayers:

- In Exodus 15:26, God said, "I am the Lord who heals you."
- Isaiah 53:4–5, a prophecy about Jesus, says He would not only die for our sins, but He would bear our sicknesses and infirmities upon Himself at the cross.
- Matthew 8:17 repeats this prophecy from Isaiah and says, "He Himself took our infirmities and bore our sicknesses."
- First Peter 2:24 says, "By [His] stripes you were healed."
- Psalm 103:2–3 says, "Bless the LORD, O my soul, and forget not all His benefits: who forgives all your iniquities, who heals all your diseases."

- Third John 1:2 (KJV) says, "Beloved, I wish above all things that thou mayest prosper and be in health, even as thy soul prospereth."

When God's Word is so clear, don't pray iffy, insecure prayers, like "God, if it is Your will, please heal me." After Jesus gave His life on the cross to pay for our healing, it doesn't honor God to say, "if it is Your will." You have to be convinced that God wants you to be healed and pray His Word from a place of faith and confidence. Instead, pray, "God, Your Word says that You are my Healer, that Jesus bore my sicknesses and infirmities upon Himself at the cross, and that I am healed by His stripes. I receive my healing by faith and ask You to manifest it in my body, in Jesus' name." The Scripture says all the promises of God are "yes" in Christ and the "Amen" is spoken by us (2 Corinthians 1:20 NIV). When we pray God's Word, we put our "Amen"—our "so be it," our agreement—on His promises. By agreeing with His Word, we give it permission to manifest in our life.

Pray the promise, not the problem. Many times, the way people pray actually does more harm than good because they are just repeating the problem. "Oh God, the doctor said such and such. God, I'm tired of being sick. I don't know why this happened to me." Praying "complainy" prayers that repeat the problem will keep you stuck where you are. Oswald Chambers said, "We have to pray with our eyes on God, not on the difficulties."[2] The purpose of prayer is not to give God your list of complaints and tell Him how bad your situation is. He already knows. He has compassion for your situation, but what moves Him to act is praying His Word back to Him in faith.

**Pray the *promise*, not the *problem*.**

## Be Persistent

The third requirement for effective prayer is *persistence*. Jesus told His disciples an important parable about a persistent widow "to make the point that at all times they ought to pray and not give up and lose heart" (Luke 18:1 AMP):

> "In a certain town there was a judge who neither feared God nor cared what people thought. And there was a widow in that town who *kept coming to him* with the plea, 'Grant me justice against my adversary.' For some time he refused. But finally he said to himself, 'Even though I don't fear God or care what people think, yet *because this widow keeps bothering me, I will see that she gets justice*, so that she won't eventually come and attack me!'" And the Lord said, "Listen to what the unjust judge says. And will not God bring about justice for his chosen ones, *who cry out to him day and night*? Will he keep putting them off?"
>
> Luke 18:2–7 NIV

So many people give up praying and believing right before their breakthrough. They start out strong after they get their diagnosis and believe God for their healing, but as time goes on and their condition worsens, they slowly start to give up. Jesus told this story to encourage us to pray without ceasing and never quit until we get our answer. It's not enough to ask God a few times and then give up. We must be like the persistent widow and keep praying as long as it takes until we get a breakthrough.

A good friend of mine attended a Christian conference some years ago. The speaker told how God had healed his eyes and given him perfect vision. At the time, my friend wore heavy prescription contact lenses. When she heard that testimony, her faith was stirred. She prayed a simple, silent prayer: "God, I know this man is a minister, but You don't love him any more than You love me. I ask You to heal my eyes, too." Nothing happened to her at the conference. There was no evidence that God even heard her prayer. At home, she continued to pray about her eyes and repeatedly thanked God by faith that they were healed. Nothing changed for two years. There was no evidence whatsoever that her prayers were doing any good. But she persisted.

One evening, she was driving to church for a meeting and singing to praise music in her car, not even thinking about her eyes. Suddenly, her vision became blurry and she could barely see. She didn't know what was happening. Fortunately, she was close to the church, and when she arrived, she removed her contact lenses. It didn't occur to her that God might have answered her prayers about her vision, so she went about her business at the church. She drove home that night without her contacts and still did not think anything about the change in her vision. The next morning when she put her contacts in, her vision was blurry. When she took them out, she finally realized she could see perfectly! Her persistence in prayer had finally paid off! When we stay in faith and persist in prayer, God will show up suddenly when we least expect it.

The enemy will do everything he can to discourage you from persisting in prayer because he doesn't want you to get healed and fulfill your destiny. Especially if you've been battling your illness for a while and your prayers haven't produced the results you hoped for, he will tell you, "Your prayers aren't working. God doesn't care about you. If He was going to heal you, He would have done it by now." Maybe it's been a while since you've even been able to hear God or sense His presence. You wonder where He is and whether He even notices you.

Everybody experiences this from time to time. David wrote in the Psalms, "Why do You stand afar off, O LORD? Why do

You hide in times of trouble?" (Psalm 10:1). "How long, O LORD? Will You forget me forever? How long will You hide Your face from me?" (Psalm 13:1). Of course, God never hides from us or forgets about us. The Bible says He will never leave nor forsake us (Hebrews 13:5). But sometimes it can feel that way.

The truth is, nobody gets immediate answers to all their prayers, and nobody feels and hears God all the time. When you took tests in school, the teacher was always silent during the test. God is always with us, but sometimes He is silent because He wants us to continue doing what we know to do and trusting Him. He is also trying to develop our spiritual muscles, character, and inner strength. He can't do that by giving us everything we ask for right away. Don't ever let the enemy or your own thoughts convince you that your prayers aren't doing any good. Your prayers are powerful, and if you don't give up, your breakthrough will come in God's perfect timing.

## Your Prayers Avail Much

The prayer of agreement with someone else or a group of people is incredibly powerful. Jesus said, "If two of you agree on earth as concerning anything that they ask, it will be done for them by My Father in heaven" (Matthew 18:19). There is great power when we join our faith with others and agree in prayer. But I want you to know that your prayers alone are just as powerful. James 5:16 says that "the effective, fervent prayer of a righteous man avails much." Not two or three or a whole group of people. God doesn't need numbers. He said just one righteous person's prayers avail much. "Avails much" means they accomplish much and have tremendous power. When you are lying on your bed all alone in the middle of the night, your prayers avail much. When there's nobody there to pray with you or encourage you, your prayers avail much. You don't need a priest, pastor, or chaplain to pray with you. That's nice, but your prayers alone avail much. You and God are enough.

When your prayers have the three key elements I discussed above—prayed with faith, based on God's Word, and offered with persistence—they will be effective and avail much. You may feel weak in every way—physically, emotionally, mentally, and even spiritually. But make no mistake: Your prayers have more power than you can fathom. As long as you are alive and can pray, you are like David with that one smooth stone he used to kill Goliath. As long as you can pray, there is hope for a miraculous turnaround.

The book of Revelation pulls back the veil and gives us an amazing peek into what happens in the spirit realm when we pray. Revelation 5:8 says that our prayers are collected in golden bowls of incense before the throne of God: "Now when He had taken the scroll, the four living creatures and the twenty-four elders fell down before the Lamb, each having a harp, and golden bowls full of incense, which are the prayers of the saints." Revelation 8:3–5 describes how an angel presents our prayers to God, and the dramatic response they have in the spirit realm:

> Then another angel, having a golden censer, came and stood at the altar. He was given much incense, that he should offer it with the prayers of all the saints upon the golden altar which was before the throne. And the smoke of the incense, with the prayers of the saints, ascended before God from the angel's hand. Then the angel took the censer, filled it with fire from the altar, and threw it to the earth. And there were noises, thunderings, lightnings, and an earthquake.

I want you to see three things from this passage. First, our prayers don't just evaporate into the atmosphere. They are collected in golden bowls of incense before the throne of God. Second, there is a powerful, cataclysmic response in heaven to our prayers. The apostle John saw thunder, lightning, and earthquakes. An angel took fire from the altar of God and threw it to the earth. God was showing John that our prayers generate a powerful response in heaven. When our prayers go up, supernatural power comes down! The third thing I want you to see is our prayers bring angelic activity. In heaven, an angel collects our prayers and presents them before the throne of God. Angels also mobilize on earth in response to our prayers. In Acts 12, Peter was put in prison for preaching the gospel, and "constant prayer was offered to God for him by the church" (Acts 12:5). A powerful angel was sent in response to those prayers and he supernaturally freed Peter from prison:

> Now behold, an angel of the Lord stood by him, and a light shone in the prison; and he struck Peter on the side and raised him up, saying, "Arise quickly!" And *his chains fell off* his hands. . . . When they were past the first and the second guard posts, they came to the iron gate that leads to the city, which *opened to them of its own accord*; and they went out and went down one street, and immediately the angel departed from him.
>
> Acts 12:7, 10

I love this story. The church prayed, an angel showed up in response to their prayers, and chains fell off Peter. God wants to break the chains of sickness off you. He wants to set you free from everything that's holding you back. Powerful angels are being dispatched to you in response to your prayers. After the chains fell off Peter, the angel caused the prison doors to open without even touching them. God is supernatural. He does things that make no sense in the natural. Jesus said He came to set the captives free, to proclaim liberty to those who are bound (Isaiah 61:1; Luke 4:18). He doesn't want you bound by sickness. Like He did for Peter, He's about to set you free from your affliction.

The Gospel of Luke tells the story of a priest named Zacharias and his wife, Elizabeth. They were elderly and had no children because Elizabeth was barren (Luke 1:5–7). One day, as Zacharias was praying in the temple, an angel appeared in response to his prayers:

> Then an angel of the Lord appeared to him, standing on the right side of the altar of incense. And when Zacharias saw him, he was troubled, and fear fell upon him. But the angel said to him, "Do not be afraid, Zacharias, for *your prayer is heard*; and your wife Elizabeth will bear you a son, and you shall call his name John. And you will have joy and gladness, and many will rejoice at his birth."
>
> Luke 1:11–14

Not only was Zacharias's prayer answered, but the baby boy he and Elizabeth had was John the Baptist, a very consequential figure in the New Testament who prepared the way for Jesus. No doubt, he and Elizabeth had been praying for many years to have a baby, because they were old at that point. It looked like it was too late in the natural, but it's never too late with God. At a time when they least expected it, God sent an angel and answered their prayers suddenly. It is another reminder to keep praying and never give up, no matter what it looks like in the natural. Your angel could show up at any time!

The book of Daniel has another fascinating story that gives another twist to angelic response to prayer. Daniel had been fasting and praying for 21 days, when suddenly an angel appeared to him and said:

> Don't be afraid, Daniel. *Since the first day you began to pray* for understanding and to humble yourself before your God, *your request has been heard in heaven. I have come in answer to your prayer.* But for twenty-one days the spirit prince of the kingdom of Persia blocked my way. Then Michael, one of the archangels, came to help me, and I left him there with the spirit prince of the kingdom of Persia.
>
> Daniel 10:12–13 NLT

The angel told Daniel that his prayer was heard the first day he prayed and that he was dispatched with the answer to it. But a demonic spirit blocked him from getting to Daniel with the answer to his prayer. The archangel Michael, captain of the angel armies of heaven, joined the battle, and the angel finally got through after 21 days. This stunning passage peels back the veil and shows that there can be demonic interference to our prayers in the spirit realm. This angel had to literally do battle with a powerful demonic spirit for 21 days and call for backup just to get through with the answer to Daniel's prayer. What if Daniel had given up and stopped praying those 21 days? His answer might not have come. That's why you have to be persistent in prayer. Refuse to give up. Show the enemy you are more determined than he is.

## The Secret of Abiding

Jesus said in John 15:7, "If you abide in Me, and My words abide in you, you will ask what you desire, and it shall be done for you." The word *abide* means to dwell there and remain, not just visit occasionally. It means to have regular fellowship and communication with the Lord. Jesus said if we have an intimate, abiding relationship with Him, we can ask whatever we want, and He will do it for us. Sounds like a great deal to me! The secret is in the abiding.

My wife and I have been married for 28 years, and since day one of our marriage, we have met in our study every morning for at least an hour to pray and read our Bibles together. This time of abiding with Christ has been the anchor for our lives and marriage. With all the trials we have been through, including many health crises of family and friends, I can't imagine not having that time of abiding with Christ every morning. But it doesn't stop there. We don't keep God in a Sunday morning or daily "quiet time" box. We pray throughout the day about everything.

Prayer is our lifeblood as believers. Like an umbilical cord connects a baby to its mother and provides everything it needs, prayer is our umbilical cord to God. But many Christians have been deceived into believing that we can get by with an anemic prayer life. I've heard prominent preachers sheepishly encourage people to try to have a fifteen-minute "quiet time" in the morning. If you spent fifteen minutes with your spouse, significant other, or child every day, how deep and meaningful do you think that relationship would be? So I encourage you to make it a nonnegotiable priority to spend some quality time with the Lord every day and develop your intimacy with Him. Then continue the dialogue with God throughout the day. Make prayer a lifestyle rather than an event. Jesus said when you abide with Him like this, you will have whatever you ask for (John 15:7).

Ideally, this time of dialoguing and abiding with Christ should involve more listening than talking on our part. The

Scripture says, "Man shall not live by bread alone, but by every word that proceeds from the mouth of God" (Matthew 4:4). God wants us to live by every word that He has for us. It may be some valuable instructions that are key to your healing. He may nudge you to forgive a certain person. Unforgiveness can be a major block to receiving healing, which I will discuss more in chapter 7. Maybe it is diet and lifestyle changes, which I will discuss in chapter 8. The listening part of prayer is easily as important as the speaking part, if not more so. God has life-changing wisdom and guidance to give us every day if we will tune our spiritual ears to receive it.

## No Distance in Prayer

What do you do when you have a loved one who is sick at home or in the hospital and you can't physically be there to pray for them, perhaps because you live in a different city or some other reason? I am writing this book during the COVID-19 pandemic; all the hospitals are locked down to visitors and even most family members. I have heard many heartbreaking stories about people who were not allowed to be with their loved ones in the hospital as they were dying. When you can't physically be with a loved one who is sick, you never have to feel helpless because there is no distance in the spirit realm. Your spiritual tools and weapons always work, regardless of distance. Your faith-filled prayers and Scripture declarations are just as powerful from a distance as they are in person.

Matthew 8 tells the story of a Roman army commander asking Jesus to heal his servant, who was at his home and close to death. Jesus said, "I will come and heal him" (Matthew 8:7). He never turned anyone away who needed healing. The commander replied, "Lord, I am not worthy that You should come under my roof. But only *speak a word*, and my servant will be healed" (Matthew 8:8). This man understood the principle I just shared: There is no distance in the spirit realm. Jesus affirmed the principles and said to the man, "Go your way; and as you have believed, so let it be done for you" (Matthew 8:13). The servant was healed without Jesus having to visit him in person. In the same way, you don't have to be physically present with someone for your prayers and Scripture declarations to work. You may not be able to be with that person, but God is. He is everywhere all the time. He will respond to your prayers and declarations—even from a distance.

## UNLOCKING HEALING WITH KEY 4: Prayers That Avail Much

Below are prayers covering healing and other needs I commonly see with those battling illness. Each prayer is almost entirely based on Scripture. As you pray these prayers in faith, God will watch over His Word to perform it, and I believe you will see supernatural breakthroughs in your situation.

### *Prayer for Your Own Healing*

*Father, You said in Exodus 15:26, "I am the Lord who heals you." You connected Your very name and identity with healing. Thank You that You are a healing God. You have the desire and the power to heal me. Nothing is impossible with You! I ask You to wash over me with Your supernatural healing power and wipe out every trace of sickness from my body. Thank You that according to Matthew 8:17 and 1 Peter 2:24, Jesus bore my sicknesses upon Himself at the cross and by His stripes I am healed. I receive Your complete healing, wholeness, and restoration in every part of my body. Psalm 103:3 says You heal all my diseases, Isaiah 54:17 says no weapon formed against me shall prosper, and Psalm 91:16 says with long life You will satisfy me. I receive all Your promises by faith with thanksgiving. Lord, You said in Mark 11:23, "Whoever says to this mountain, 'Be removed and be cast into the sea,' and does not doubt in his heart, but believes for those things he says will be done, will have whatever he says." So I speak to every sickness, disease, pain, and symptom and command it to be removed from my body in the name of Jesus. I speak healing, wholeness, and restoration to every part of my body and cover every cell in my body with the healing, delivering blood of the Lord Jesus Christ. I declare that I will live out all my days in divine health, vim, vigor, vitality, energy, and strength by the shed blood of Jesus and the power of the Holy Spirit. Thank You, Lord, for healing me. Thank You that I will live a long, healthy, satisfying life and my best days are still in front of me. I pray all these things in the all-powerful, matchless name of Jesus, Amen.*

### Prayer for a Loved One's Healing

*Father, thank You that [name loved one/friend] is Your child, You love him/her even more than I do, and You have him/her in the palm of Your mighty hand. Thank You that You are his/her Healer, Deliverer, Strengthener, and everything he/she needs. Lord, You have all power, and nothing is too hard for You. I ask You to touch [name] from the top of his/her head to the bottom of his/her feet with Your mighty healing power. Wipe out every trace of sickness and disease [name anything else specific here—cancer, infection, etc.] from his/her body and restore him/her completely to health. You promised in Psalm 103:3 to heal [name] of all his/her diseases. You said no weapon formed against him/her would prosper and with long life You would satisfy him/her and show him/her Your salvation. I declare over him/her Matthew 8:17 and 1 Peter 2:24—that Jesus bore his/her sicknesses and infirmities upon Himself at the cross and by His stripes he/she is healed. He/she will live out all his/her days in divine health, vim, vigor, vitality, energy, and strength by the shed blood of Jesus and the power of the Holy Spirit. I cover every cell in his/her body with the blood of Jesus and speak healing, wholeness, and restoration over every part of his/her body. I declare that he/she will live and not die to declare the works of the Lord, according to Psalm 118:17. Father, You said the prayer of faith will save the sick and You will raise them up (James 5:15). Thank You for hearing my prayer of faith and completely healing [their name]. I give You all the praise, glory, and honor for it, and it's in the matchless name of Jesus I pray all these things, Amen.*

### Prayer for Doctors, Nurses, and Other Care Providers

*Father God, thank You for every doctor, nurse, healthcare worker, social worker, chaplain, pastor, and everyone else involved in my care. I ask You to give them Your supernatural wisdom, guidance, and anointing so they can give me and others the best care possible. [If you need surgery: Father, I ask You to guide the surgeon's hands. Anoint him/her and all those assisting in the surgery and help them to perform the surgery flawlessly.] When they are feeling weary and need encouragement, pour Your grace upon them and send angels to minister to them. Bless them in every area of their lives, keep them healthy, provide for all their needs, and protect them and their families. I pray that if any of them do not know Jesus as their Lord and Savior, You would reveal Yourself to them and they would receive salvation in Christ. Help me to be a good witness to them and to be bold about sharing my faith when You prompt me to. In Jesus' precious name, Amen.*

### Prayer to Overcome Fear and Anxiety

*Father, Your Word says You have not given me a spirit of fear, but of power, love, and a sound mind (2 Timothy 1:7). Fear is not from You. Fear is from the enemy and has no place in my life. I reject and resist fear in all its forms and command it to go from me now, in the mighty name of Jesus. I cast down every fearful thought and imagination from my mind, in Jesus' name. God, I thank You that Your perfect love casts out all fear from me (1 John 4:18). I receive Your perfect love for me right now. Wash over me with Your love. Give me a deep, abiding sense of Your unfailing love for me that extinguishes all fear and anxiety. Lord, Your Word commands us to "be anxious for nothing, but in everything by prayer and supplication, with thanksgiving, let your requests be made known to God; and the peace of God, which surpasses all understanding, will guard your heart and mind through Christ Jesus" (Philippians 4:6). I choose to give You my anxieties and fears, and I thank You that Your supernatural peace will guard my heart and mind from vexing thoughts and emotions.*

*Father, You commanded us to "be strong and of good courage. Do not be afraid; nor be dismayed, for the* LORD *your God will be with you wherever you go" (Joshua 1:9). Help me to be strong and of good courage. Strengthen me with all might by Your Spirit in my inner man (Ephesians 3:16). Thank You that that I have no reason to fear because You are with me and for me wherever I go. You have me in the palm of Your hand. You are fighting my battles for me and subduing my enemies before me (Psalm 18:39). No weapon formed against me shall prosper (Isaiah 54:17). In all things I am more than a conqueror through Christ who loves me (Romans 8:37). You always cause me to triumph in Christ Jesus (2 Corinthians 2:14). Help me to have no fear, anxiety, or worry, and to totally rest and trust in You. In the precious name of Jesus I pray, Amen.*

### Prayer for Encouragement and Hope

*Father, Your Word says, "May the God of hope fill you with all joy and peace in believing, that you may abound in hope by the power of the Holy Spirit" (Romans 15:13). I ask You to fill me with Your supernatural joy and peace and cause me to abound in hope by the power of Your Spirit. Thank You that You are the God of all hope. There is always hope in You because You are for me and have a great plan for my life. You have all power, and nothing is impossible with You. You can turn any situation around with one touch. I ask You to encourage my heart today and renew my hope and strength. Lord, I repent of all fear, self-pity, discouragement, and doubt, and for believing any lies of the enemy. I reject any thoughts and emotions that don't line up with Your Word. I command all fear, discouragement, hopelessness, depression, oppression, doubt, and anything else that is not from God to go from me now in the name of Jesus and not to come back!*

*Lord, thank You that in all things I am more than a conqueror. You always cause me to triumph in Christ Jesus. You are singing songs of deliverance over me. No weapon formed against me will ever prosper. Help me to have a victorious mindset. Help me to think, talk, and act like more than a conqueror in Christ Jesus. Lord, Your Word commands me to cast all my cares [anxieties, worries, and concerns] once and for all on You because You care about me [with deepest affection and watch over me carefully]* (1 Peter 5:7 AMP)*. So right now I cast all my burdens, cares, concerns, fears, feelings of hopelessness, worries, anxieties, sorrows, doubts, discouragement, and depression on You. I release them to You and ask You to replace them with Your joy and peace. Father, thank You that Your joy and peace are the fruit of the Holy Spirit, who lives inside me, and they don't depend on circumstances. Thank You that Your joy is my strength and Your peace guards my heart and mind through Christ Jesus. I let go of everything trying to steal my joy and peace, and I tap in to Your supernatural joy and peace right now. According to Psalm 23, You restore my soul, Your rod and staff comfort me in the valleys of life, and Your goodness and mercy follow me all the days of my life. You've given Your angels charge over me (Psalm 11). Thank You for that! Help me to be encouraged and full of hope as I trust You with my life and healing. I pray all these things in the mighty name of Jesus, Amen.*

### Prayer against Doubt and for More Faith

*Father, I come to You today confessing that I am struggling with doubt. Thank You that Your Word says there is no condemnation for those who are in Christ Jesus, so I don't have to feel guilty or condemned because I have doubts. Some of the greatest people in the Bible struggled with doubt at times. Your Word tells about a man who came to You to heal his son, who had seizures since childhood. He said, "Lord, I believe; help my unbelief!" (Mark 9:24). Despite his having some unbelief, You had mercy on him and healed his son. I come to You today with the same cry: Help my unbelief! Part of me believes You for my healing, but part of me struggles with unbelief. I ask You to remove all unbelief and doubt from me. Renew a steadfast spirit and faith within me. Lord, You said that all things are possible if I can believe, and that if I have a mustard seed of faith, nothing will be impossible. Help me to have the faith I need to receive my healing. Help me to believe You more than I believe the doctors and medicine, the natural facts, and my own thoughts and emotions. When I feel weak in my faith, I ask You to revive, refresh, and strengthen my faith. Help me to have tough, determined, never-say-die faith. Guard my heart and mind from fear, worry, doubt, lies, and anything else that would undermine my faith. Help me to take steps every day to feed my faith and unleash its power. God, I confess that You have all power and are well able to heal me. I believe You for my complete healing, wholeness, and restoration. In Jesus' mighty name, Amen.*

### *Prayer for Good Sleep*

*Heavenly Father, Your Word promises that I will lie down in peace and my sleep will be sweet (Psalm 4:8; Proverbs 3:24). You also promised that You are watching over me while I sleep (Psalm 3:5). Thank You for blessing me tonight with sweet, peaceful, refreshing, deep, uninterrupted sleep and good dreams. Just as You supernaturally caused Adam to fall into a deep sleep when You removed his rib, cause deep sleep to come upon me all night and let me awake tomorrow feeling refreshed, rested, and ready to serve You. I pray that even if nurses come in during the night and medical devices make noise, I will sleep like a baby. I ask You to remove any pain or discomfort from my body, anxious thoughts from my mind, or anything else that would disrupt my sleep. I ask You to give Your mighty warring and defending angels charge over me while I sleep, according to Psalm 91:11–12. Put Your hedge of protection around me on all sides so that the enemy cannot penetrate. I cover myself, my sleep, my dreams, and my room with the blood of Jesus. Lord, You said in Luke 10:19 that You have given me authority over all the power of the enemy. So I command every spirit of insomnia, restlessness, anxiety, torment, and every other spirit that would try to interrupt my sleep to go from me, in the name of Jesus. I bind, cut off, cancel, and nullify every demonic assignment and attack against me and my sleep, in Jesus' name. I invite the presence of the Holy Spirit into my room right now and ask for the Spirit of the living God to brood over me while I sleep. Thank You, Father, for a great night's sleep tonight. I receive it by faith with thanksgiving.*

*I pray all these things in the precious name of Jesus, Amen.*

### Prayer against Depression

*Father, thank You that Jesus died not only for my sins, but to set me free from every stronghold, bondage, generational curse, and yoke of oppression. In Christ, I am free from everything that would try to hold me back from God's best in my life. I praise You that in Christ I am a brand-new creation (2 Corinthians 5:17). Old things have passed away and all things have become new (2 Corinthians 5:17). Old generational sin patterns, bad habits, destructive ways of thinking and behaving; past mistakes, failures, hurts, and offenses have all passed away. I am a new creation in Christ. Thank You, Lord, that You have given me the oil of joy for mourning and the garment of praise for the spirit of heaviness (Isaiah 61:3). Thank You that I have the fruit of joy and peace that comes from the Holy Spirit (Galatians 5:22). By the shed blood of Jesus and Your Holy Spirit, I am free from all depression, anxiety, fear, worry, sadness, discouragement, despair, and self-pity. Lord, You said in Luke 10:19 that You have given me authority over all the power of the enemy. So I command every spirit of heaviness, depression, discouragement, and despair to go from me and not to return, in the mighty name of Jesus. I break all heaviness, depression, and discouragement off me, in Jesus' name. Lord, according to Isaiah 61:3, I ask You to give me the oil of joy for mourning and the garment of praise for the spirit of heaviness. I praise You because You are good all the time, even when my circumstances are not good. You are my Healer, Deliverer, and Strengthener. You are the glory and the lifter of my head (Psalm 3:3b). Your plans for me are good, to give me a hope and a future. You always cause me to triumph in Christ Jesus. You have made me more than a conqueror in all things by Christ Jesus. You are singing songs of deliverance over me (Psalm 32:7). You are delivering me out of all my troubles (Psalm 34:17). My best days and greatest victories are in my future, not my past (Proverbs 4:18). So I reject, renounce, and refuse all depression, heaviness, discouragement, and despair, and I receive God's supernatural joy, peace, and encouragement, in the mighty, matchless name of Jesus, Amen.*

### *Prayer for Finances*

*Father, thank You that You are Jehovah Jireh, the Lord my Provider (Genesis 22:14). You are my Shepherd; I shall not lack (Psalm 23:1). You promised in Philippians 4:19 to supply all my needs according to Your riches in glory by Christ Jesus. You said in Deuteronomy 28 that You are commanding the blessing upon my storehouse, opening Your good treasure to me, and bringing me increase and abundance. Father, I look to You and You alone for my provision, not my bank account, employer, insurance company, or anything else. Those are resources, but You are my Source. Father, I ask You to remove all lack from my life and to provide for every financial need I have. The earth is Yours and the fullness thereof (Psalm 24:1). You own the cattle on a thousand hills (Psalm 50:10). Everything in heaven and earth belongs to You. You have an endless supply. There is no lack with You, no matter what the economy is doing or what my circumstances are. You are not limited by my bank account or anything else in the natural. You have supernatural ways of providing for my needs that I haven't even thought about. You multiplied the widow's oil and caused it never to run dry (1 Kings 17:8–16). You multiplied five loaves and two fish so there was enough to feed more than five thousand people and with twelve baskets left over (Matthew 14:13–21). Jesus told Peter to look in a fish's mouth and there was a coin in it to pay His taxes (Matthew 17:24–27). Lord, deliver me from a poverty and lack mindset and stretch my faith to believe You for supernatural provision. Help me not to have any fear, worry, or anxiety about finances, but to totally trust You. According to Your Word, I break all poverty, lack, and debt off my life, in the mighty name of Jesus. I declare that God is supplying all my needs, my finances are blessed and abounding, and there is no lack in my life. Father, I receive all Your promises of provision and prosperity by faith with thanksgiving, and I pray all these things in the name above every name—Jesus Christ, Amen.*

### Prayer for Wisdom in Health-Care Decisions

*Father, You said in James 1:5 (NIV), "If any of you lacks wisdom, you should ask God, who gives generously to all without finding fault, and it will be given to you." You said in Psalm 32:8 (NIV), "I will instruct you and teach you in the way you should go; I will counsel you with my loving eye on you." I come to You today asking for wisdom and guidance in all decisions regarding my health care. Help me to be led by Your Spirit and discern Your will in every decision I make. Your Word says You are not the author of confusion, but You are a very clear and precise God. I pray You would remove all confusion and doubt from my mind and make every decision crystal clear. I ask You to give my doctors wisdom in every decision they make regarding my care. Thank You for Your wisdom and guidance as I navigate the path to complete healing, wholeness, and restoration. In Jesus' precious name I pray. Amen.*

KEY 5

# Praise Precedes the Victory

> Heal me, LORD, and I will be healed . . . for you are the one I praise.
>
> Jeremiah 17:14 NIV

> Complain and remain. Praise and be raised.
>
> Joyce Meyer

YOU MAY NEVER HAVE THOUGHT about praising God this way, but it is one of the most powerful weapons in your arsenal for healing. It is an often-underutilized superpower that can change everything. Many people think praise is just something we do in church while the worship team is singing or after God does something amazing in our lives. Certainly, we praise God in those times, but the most important time to praise Him is in the valley, not on the mountaintop. Anybody can praise God on the mountaintop when everything is going their way, but the true test is whether we can praise Him in the dark, wilderness seasons of life. It is when nothing is going right in our lives but we lift our eyes to heaven and say, "God, even though nothing is going my way right now, You are good all the time. Father, even though I don't understand, I trust You. I know You love me and Your plans for me are good. I know You are a just and merciful God and You promised to work all things together for my good." In these times, praise has the power to shift the atmosphere, usher in the presence of God, and produce a miracle breakthrough. Don't wait for God to do something before you praise Him. Praise *precedes* the victory!

Nowhere is this clearer than in the story of the apostle Paul and Silas being imprisoned in Acts 16. First, they were arrested for preaching the gospel, stripped naked, and publicly beaten. It was a very painful and bloody ordeal. Then, without any treatment of their wounds, they were thrown into the innermost part of the prison, where it was dark, damp, and unbearably cold. The lack of proper indoor plumbing created a horrible stench. On top of that, they were made to wear painful shackles on their ankles and placed in a cramped cell with many other prisoners. It was the most miserable scene you can imagine. I don't know about you, but there wouldn't be one shred of me that would feel like praising God in that situation. In fact, if I'm honest, I would be angry. I would probably think, *God, how could You let this happen? I was doing my best to serve You. This is so unfair!*

But Paul kept a good attitude and used his time in that Philippian prison to write the book of Philippians, where he said, "Whatever is worthy of praise, let your mind dwell on these things" (Philippians 4:8). Even in the midst of this horrible, unfair situation, Paul found things to praise God about.

One evening at around midnight, Paul and Silas were praying and singing hymns. Instead of being discouraged and complaining, they praised God. What happened next is a testament to the awesome power of praise. "Suddenly there was a great earthquake, so that the foundations of the prison were shaken; and immediately all the doors were opened and everyone's chains were loosed" (Acts 16:26). Their praise touched the heart of God and produced that miracle. Not only were they freed from prison, but the warden and his family were saved and baptized. If you want to get God's attention, start praising Him! If you need to be freed from the chains of sickness and disease, start praising Him! Like Paul and Silas, you can turn your hospital room or home into a place of praise.

Praise is acknowledging who God is, regardless of our circumstances. He breathed life into us. He sent Jesus to die for us and gave us eternal life. He loves us with a perfect, unconditional love. He has all power and the answer to every problem we face. He is perfect and holy. Praise is magnifying God and making Him bigger and more important than anything else in our lives. It is lifting our heart and hands to God and surrendering to His perfect will.

## Shift Your Atmosphere

We have all been in a room where two people are arguing, and the atmosphere is very tense. There's a saying: "You could have cut the tension with a knife." We have a spiritual atmosphere around us that is influenced by our words, attitudes, and actions. Often when I walk into a patient's room, the window blinds are closed, and the room is dark.

The patient usually has a game show, soap opera, or something similar on the TV. The walls are often bare except for a whiteboard with medical information scrawled on it. The atmosphere in the room usually feels clinical, spiritually dead, and even oppressive at times. I get it: Hospitals are clinical and institutional, and being sick is not a happy occasion. This makes what I'm about to tell you even more important. If you are going to win the battle for your health, you have to do something proactive every day to shift the atmosphere in your room so it attracts the presence of God and His miracles. Nothing does that better than praise.

Psalm 22:3 says God *inhabits* the praises of His people. Think about that: Wherever there is praise, God's presence is there. When God shows up, anything is possible. Miracles happen in His presence, like the story of Paul and Silas I shared earlier. God's presence is ushered in by your praises. The more you praise Him, the more His presence will flood your room and shift the atmosphere. You will feel refreshed, revived, and strengthened, and your faith will be renewed. The Scripture says refreshing times come from the presence of the Lord and that in His presence is fullness of joy (Acts 3:19; Psalm 16:11).

If you are taking care of a loved one who is sick, one of the best things you can do is fill their room or home with praise. You can play some praise and worship music on your phone or laptop. While I was writing this chapter, my brother-in-law, who had a massive stroke a few years ago, had a medical emergency and had to be rushed to the emergency room. He was unconscious, his blood pressure was 60/40-something, he was vomiting blood, and they said he had sepsis, a life-threatening blood infection. When my wife and I went to pray for him in the ER, he was on a ventilator and the situation was very dire. We prayed and declared the Word of God over him, and then I got my phone out and turned on a praise song. You could feel the whole atmosphere immediately shift. The heaviness and foreboding that hung in the air lifted. As God is my witness, his blood pressure went up twenty points while we praised God. Not only that, but his right leg, which had been completely paralyzed for two years, started moving. It was amazing! My brother-in-law made nothing short of a miraculous recovery over the next two days and was released from the hospital.

I heard a powerful testimony about a little boy who drowned in the ocean while on a family vacation. His father saw his lifeless body floating in the surf and pulled him out. His body had turned blue, and he had no pulse. For several minutes, the family did CPR on him to no avail. Two nurses happened to be nearby and came over to help perform CPR. Still no pulse. Precious minutes went by without any sign of life. Suddenly, the daughter lifted her hands and started singing the praise song "Raise a Hallelujah." She sang the chorus over and over about praising God in the middle of the storm and hope rising out of the ashes.

The mother, who was desperately praying over her son, said the moment her daughter started praising God, it was like a bolt of electricity. Praise gets the attention of heaven! Shortly afterward, the boy's pulse suddenly returned. He was still unconscious and taken to a hospital 45 minutes away. Doctors were concerned that he would be brain damaged after being deprived of oxygen for so long. But a few days later, the boy woke up with no brain damage whatsoever.[1]

Praise changes everything. It shifts the atmosphere. It invites God's presence and miracles. Had that boy's sister not made the critical decision to start praising God during the most gut-wrenching, stressful moment of her life, it is doubtful her brother would be alive and well today.

Like that sister and like Paul and Silas in prison, you can praise God even when you don't feel like it. The Bible calls this giving God the "sacrifice of praise" (Hebrews 13:15; Jeremiah 33:11). It is praising God when nothing in your flesh wants to do so. In fact, you may feel like doing the opposite of praising God. That's why it's called a sacrifice. Your emotions and circumstances don't have to control you. You can offer God the sacrifice of praise because He is good at all times. Your circumstances may not be good, but God is good. You can offer Him the sacrifice of praise to show Him you believe in Him, trust Him, and surrender to His perfect will.

**Praise changes everything. It shifts the atmosphere. It invites God's presence and miracles.**

## Praise Activates and Releases Our Faith

Praise stirs your faith because it causes you to focus on God instead of your problems. It helps you look beyond your problems, focus on the Solution, and magnify God above all else. When you do that, you are not denying your problems; you are acknowledging that God is greater than any situation you face.

Andrew Wommack, a great television Bible teacher, told how he and his wife had gotten home from a trip at around 2:00 one morning. Just as they were going to bed about 4 a.m., they got a call from one of their sons saying that their other son, Peter, had died unexpectedly. He told them to go to the hospital in Colorado Springs, Colorado. Andrew and his wife live in the countryside about an hour away, so they had a lot of time to think about things on their way. They felt grief and shock, just as any parents would after getting a call like that, but they decided to do something radical on the drive to the hospital. Philippians 4:4 kept resonating in Andrew's spirit: "Rejoice in the Lord always. Again, I will say, rejoice!" He and his wife decided to start praising God in the middle of their worst nightmare.

The world tells us we should be hysterical and grief-stricken in situations like that, but God's Word tells us to rejoice always, no matter what we are going through. Andrew and his wife praised God for almost an hour: "God, You are a good God. You didn't take our son from us. Your ways and Your plans are perfect. You created our son and love him even more than we do. We trust You, even when we don't understand." On and on, they turned their focus to God and praised Him for everything they could think of regarding their son. As they did that, a strange peace came over them. They were not grief-stricken or shaken. They knew God was on the throne and in control. Their faith was stirred up to believe for the impossible as they declared the goodness and faithfulness of God.

When they finally arrived at the hospital, the son who had called them with the news ran up and told them Peter had suddenly sat up and was talking after being dead for nearly five hours. He had been pronounced dead by a physician, stripped naked, and moved to a refrigerated morgue with a toe tag on. He not only came back to life but had no brain damage! What an amazing miracle and testament to the power of praise!

## Praise Is a Weapon

The Scripture says God is "*fearful in praises*" (Exodus 15:11). One of my favorite stories in the Bible perfectly illustrates what this means. In 2 Chronicles 20, King Jehoshaphat and the people of Judah were surrounded on all sides by three enemy armies. Jehoshaphat gathered the people to fast, pray, and seek God. He prayed a powerful prayer, in which he said, "For we have no power against this great multitude that is coming against us; nor do we know what to do, but our eyes are upon You" (2 Chronicles 20:12). I love that: "We don't know what to do, but our eyes are on You." I've had to pray that many times myself. You may feel that way too as you battle your medical condition, but do what Jehoshaphat did and keep your eyes on God. Then the people turned their attention away from the crisis and started worshiping God: "The [people] stood up to praise the LORD God of Israel with voices loud and high" (2 Chronicles 20:19). These people were facing annihilation, and they responded by praising God with all their might. The next morning, they woke up early to face the enemy, and King Jehoshaphat "appointed those who should sing to the LORD, and who should praise the beauty of holiness, as they went out before the army and were saying: 'Praise the LORD, for His mercy endures forever'" (2 Chronicles 20:21).

Have you ever heard of a leader sending a praise team out to face enemy armies? In the natural, that sounds like a crazy battle strategy. But what happened next was breathtaking. As the people were praising God, it says "the LORD set ambushes against the people of Ammon, Moab, and Mount Seir, who had come against Judah; and they were defeated" (2 Chronicles 20:22). It goes on to say the Lord caused the three armies to fight against each other until they were annihilated, without the people of Judah having to lift a finger! That is God being fearful in praises. Not only that, but the people of Judah took many valuables, precious jewelry, and other spoils from the enemy. No matter what enemy you are facing in your body or life, just begin to praise and worship God, and He will fight your battles for you.

Another well-known story from the Bible that demonstrates how God is fearful in praises is the battle of Jericho. After Moses' death, Joshua assumed the role as leader of the Israelites and took them into the Promised Land. The first enemies they encountered there were in Jericho, a fortified town with very high, thick walls. Archeologists have said the stone walls were about six feet thick and up to seventeen feet high. The Israelites had wandered in the wilderness for forty years after being slaves in Egypt and certainly were not prepared to defeat a fortified city like Jericho. But the Lord told Joshua to have the people march around the city quietly once a day for six days. On the seventh day, He told Joshua to send the priests with the ark of the covenant and rams' horns ahead of the people, to march around the city quietly seven times, and on the seventh lap to let out a shout of praise to the Lord.

When the Israelites rounded Jericho the seventh time, the priests blew the rams' horns and the people shouted as loud as they could. They did not lift a finger to fight; they just praised God with all their might. God responded to their praise with one of the most astonishing miracles in the Bible. He caused the mighty walls of Jericho to fall down flat! If you want God to show up and do an amazing miracle in your life, if you need Him to fight your battles and knock down the walls of sickness in your life, give Him praise every day!

## Magnify God above Your Sickness

The word *magnify* means "to make bigger." We can't make God bigger than He already is, but to magnify Him means we make Him bigger in our own life and circumstances.

Unfortunately, I often see people who are battling illness magnify their illness and make it the center of their focus. I have seen many become consumed with their condition until it is almost all they think and talk about. The same people who do this also tend to magnify whatever the doctors say as if their word is gospel and they have the final say. I'm encouraging you to keep your focus on God and magnify Him over your illness and the doctors. God is so much bigger than your illness, and He has all power. The doctors don't have the final say; God does. God uses doctors and medicine, but He alone is your Healer.

In the Bible story about Peter walking on the water, Peter was able to defy the law of gravity and do the impossible as long as he kept his eyes on Jesus (Matthew 14:22–31). But at one point he shifted his focus away from Jesus to the boisterous winds and waves (i.e., the natural circumstances). He became afraid and began to sink. When you focus on your illness instead of God and listen to what the doctors say more than what God says, it will cause you to operate in fear instead of faith. You'll begin to sink like Peter did into discouragement, depression, and doubt. Don't focus on the bigness of your problem; focus on the bigness of God. Your sickness may seem big and scary, but it's no match for our God. He's bigger than any sickness or circumstance.

**Don't focus on the bigness of your *problem*; focus on the bigness of *God*.**

When David was just a teenage boy and faced the giant Goliath in battle, his situation looked hopeless. Goliath was over nine feet tall, dressed in full body armor, and armed with a giant sword and a long spear. He also had an armor-bearer who went before him with a large shield to protect him (1 Samuel 17:41). David was much smaller, had no armor, and was armed with only a slingshot and a few rocks. When Goliath saw how small and unprepared David was, he started cursing him. He said, "Am I a dog that you come to me with sticks? . . . Come to me, and I will give your flesh to the birds of the air and the beasts of the field!" (1 Samuel 17:43–44). I don't know about you, but I would have been pretty terrified and intimidated to be in David's position. Maybe when you look at your illness, it looks like a lopsided, hopeless battle. Maybe the enemy is telling you that you're not going to make it, like Goliath told David.

But I love David's response. Rather than focusing on the size of the snarling, frightening giant threatening to kill him, David focused on the size of his God. He told Goliath:

> You come to me with a sword, with a spear, and with a javelin. But *I come to you in the name of the LORD of hosts*, the God of the armies of Israel, whom you have defied. This day *the LORD will deliver you into my hand*, and I will strike you and take your head from you. And this day I will give the carcasses of the camp of the Philistines to the birds of the air and the wild beasts of the earth, that all the earth may know that there is a God in Israel. Then all this assembly shall know that the LORD does not save with sword and spear; for *the battle is the LORD's, and He will give you into our hands.*
>
> 1 Samuel 17:45–47

Notice that David never called Goliath a giant. When you allow something to become big in your mind, you give it permission to be on the throne of your life. Take your sickness, the doctors, and anything else besides God off the throne of your life. Only God belongs there. David didn't magnify Goliath's size; he magnified the size of his God. He said, "I come to you in the name of the LORD. . . . The LORD will deliver you into my hand. . . . The battle is the LORD's." Magnifying the size and power of God gave him the courage he needed to defeat Goliath. In fact, David *ran* toward Goliath, flung a rock from his slingshot at him, and struck him to the ground. Then he took the giant's own sword and cut his head off.

When you keep your focus on God and magnify Him above all else, you can defeat any giant in your life. Every day, say, "God, I praise You. I magnify You. You are far bigger and more powerful than this sickness or problem I face. I don't magnify this sickness. I don't magnify doctors or medicine. I magnify You alone. You alone are on the throne of my life. I take my focus off my situation and fix my gaze on You, the Author and Finisher of my faith. You are God Almighty and You have all power and authority. You are fighting my battles and defeating every giant in my life. You always lead me to triumph in Christ Jesus and will bring me out of this challenging situation with the victory. I praise You!"

## Thankfulness

Whereas praise is extolling God for *who He is*, thankfulness is being grateful for *what He's done*. Thankfulness is just as important as praise. On the journey to your healing, you are likely to experience many small victories along the way—an amazing doctor or nurse God brings your way, people He sends to encourage and pray for you, an appointment that suddenly opens with a doctor who was booked for months, a positive test result or response to treatment, or spiritual revelations God gives you. If you pay attention, God will reveal His presence and goodness to you in countless ways. The Scripture says, "Every good gift and every perfect gift is from above, and comes down from the Father. . . ." (James

1:17). When you receive anything good, it's not just a lucky break or coincidence. That's God showing you His goodness and favor. All He wants is to be thanked, like we like to be thanked when we do something nice for someone. I don't think we can ever thank God too much.

The story of ten lepers that Jesus healed shows how important and powerful thankfulness is:

> Then as He entered a certain village, there met Him ten men who were lepers, who stood afar off. And they lifted up their voices and said, "Jesus, Master, have mercy on us!" So when He saw them, He said to them, "Go, show yourselves to the priests." And so it was that as they went, they were cleansed. And one of them, when he saw that he was healed, returned, and *with a loud voice glorified God, and fell down on his face at His feet, giving Him thanks*. And he was a Samaritan. So Jesus answered and said, "Were there not ten cleansed? But where are the nine? Were there not any found who returned to give glory to God except this foreigner?" And He said to him, "Arise, go your way. Your faith has made you well."
>
> Luke 17:12–19

It's interesting that these ten lepers "lifted up their voices" and cried out to Jesus for healing, but only one came back and lifted up his voice to *thank* Jesus after being healed. Jesus asked the thankful leper why the other nine did not return to give Him thanks. It is clear that He wanted and expected to be thanked. Notice how Jesus gave an extra blessing to the one leper who returned to give thanks. The King James translation says He made him "whole." In the original Greek of the New Testament, the word used here is *sozo*, which means "to save, to make whole in every way." The other lepers received a physical healing, but Jesus gave the thankful leper the added blessing of complete wholeness in his soul that was deeper than just the physical healing.[2] *God blesses a thankful spirit*. Like He did with this leper, He not only wants to heal you physically; He wants to make you whole in every way and bless you with an abundant life (John 10:10). Be like this one leper and thank God for every positive thing that happens in your life, no matter how small. Living with an attitude of gratitude will help usher in His supernatural health and wholeness in your entire being.

In 1 Thessalonians 5:18, Paul said "in *everything* give thanks; for this is the will of God in Christ Jesus for you." He didn't say give thanks *for* everything. You don't have to thank God for your sickness or problem. Paul said *in* everything give thanks. That's because no matter how bad your situation is, there are always many things to be thankful for. Instead of focusing on what hasn't gone your way and what you're discouraged about, focus on what you're thankful for. Seeds of discouragement cannot take root in a thankful heart.

Thankfulness is a mindset and a habit. Make up your mind to live with an attitude of gratitude. The more thankful you are, the more you'll find to be thankful for. Negativity is also a mindset and a habit. The more negative you are, the more you'll find to be negative about.

**Seeds of *discouragement* cannot take root in a *thankful* heart.**

In Old Testament times, leaders would stack memorial stones in a place where God did something great for them. These stones served as a reminder to be thankful for what God had done. For example, in Joshua 4 God did a powerful miracle and parted the Jordan River so the people could cross over into the Promised Land. Joshua ordered that a stack of twelve stones representing the twelve tribes of Israel be placed in that spot as a memorial of what God did.

In the same way, we need to have memorial stones in our lives. I encourage you to keep a gratitude journal and write down every blessing God brings you, small and large. Every journal entry will be a memorial stone to help you remember what God has done in your life. Over time, we tend to forget all the little things God does for us on a daily basis, if we don't write them down. If you don't feel like writing, you can dictate into the Notes app on your phone and it will type it for you.

My wife and I have kept a gratitude journal for twenty years. It is now several volumes long. It's amazing to look back and see everything God has done that we'd forgotten about. When we are going through a trial and feel discouraged, we pull out our gratitude journal and remind ourselves of God's goodness and faithfulness and the countless ways He has blessed us. Every time we do this, it instantly lifts our spirits and shifts our perspective. There is no greater remedy for discouragement than reminding yourself of what God has done in your life and being grateful.

If you are not in a thankful frame of mind or can't think of anything to be thankful for, start with the basics: "Father, I thank You for the breath in my lungs. Thank You for my eternal salvation in Christ Jesus. Thank You that I live in a free country with the best health care in the world. Thank You for my family, friends, church, and all those who love me. Thank You for my doctors, nurses, and every person who has cared for me." This will prime the pump of thankfulness and help you think of more things to give God thanks for. There have been times in my own life when I was so discouraged and couldn't seem to snap out of it that I got out a notebook and started writing down everything I could think of that I was thankful for. I forced myself to focus on all the good in my life and what I had instead of what I didn't have. This simple exercise was so powerful that it shifted my whole perspective. As I practiced thankfulness, my heaviness departed and I felt encouraged, strengthened, and revived. If you will live with this attitude of gratitude, you will keep yourself strong and positive. You will fend off discouragement and despair. And you will attract more of God's blessings, including your healing.

### *Prayer of Praise and Thanksgiving*

*Father God, Your Word says in Psalm 100:4, "Enter into His gates with thanksgiving, and into His courts with praise. Be thankful to Him, and bless His name." Father, I praise You because You are good all the time. You are holy, perfect, and majestic in all Your ways. You are great and greatly to be praised. You have all power and authority in heaven and on earth. You love me with perfect love, and nothing can separate me from Your love. You are full of grace and mercy, and Your compassions never fail. You are my Salvation, Healer, Strength, Deliverer, Comforter, Protector, and Provider. You are everything I need. I praise You for all that You are in my life. I return, like that one leper, to thank You for all that You've done in my life. I thank You for all the victories, small and large; all the things You have protected me from; all the wonderful people You have brought into my life; and all the blessings You have given me. [Thank Him for any blessings you want to specifically mention.] Father, I thank You by faith that my healing is on the way. Thank You that Your plans for me are good, to give me a hope and a future (Jeremiah 29:11). Thank You that according to Your Word, my path is like the sun, shining brighter and brighter (Proverbs 4:18). Thank You that my brightest days and greatest victories are in my future, not my past. Help me to live with an attitude of gratitude, and let Your praises be continually in my mouth so my healing will come and I will live the abundant life Jesus died to give me (Psalm 34:1; John 10:10). In Jesus' name, Amen.*

## UNLOCKING HEALING WITH KEY 5: The Names of God and Names of Jesus

Below, I have provided for you a list of most of the names of God and Jesus in the Bible. Each name reveals something significant about God's nature and how He operates in our lives. Psalm 105:1 says, "Give praise to the LORD, *proclaim His name*." This verse and many others talk about the power of proclaiming God's name. When you praise God, you can call Him by these names to remind yourself and praise Him for all that He is and does in your life.

## Names of God

| Name | Meaning & Application | Scriptures |
|---|---|---|
| Father | One of the greatest things Jesus did on earth was to reveal God as our heavenly Father. When teaching about God, He used the phrase "your Father" almost thirty times in the Gospels. Every time but one that Jesus addressed God, He called Him "Father." When He taught us the Lord's Prayer, He said to address God as "Our Father who is in heaven." He wanted us to understand that God is not just the Creator of the universe or a "higher power"; He is our loving Father. God had many names in the Old Testament, but the name "Father" is perhaps His greatest name and encompasses all the others. It lets us know that we are His children and that He wants to be intimately involved in our lives. First John 3:1 says, "See what great love the Father has lavished on us, that we should be called children of God" (NIV). | Matthew 5:16; 6:6, 9; John 6:46; 2 Corinthians 1:3; 6:18; 1 John 3:1 |
| Abba | The name *Abba* used in Romans 8:15 means "Daddy." God is not just our God and our Father; He is our Daddy. When someone calls their father "Daddy" or "Dad," it is more intimate and casual. By giving Himself this name, God was saying, "You don't have to approach Me in a formal, religious way. I am not a distant, impersonal God. I am your Daddy, and you are My beloved child. I want to be involved in the details of your life. You can come crawl up in My lap and talk to Me about anything." This is God's heart toward us. | Romans 8:15 |
| Jehovah Rapha | *The God Who Heals You*<br>When God called Himself this name, He connected His very name and identity with healing. Healing is not just something He does; it is who He is! He wants to heal not only our bodies, but also our souls, relationships, and everything in our lives. | Exodus 15:26 |
| Jehovah Shammah | *The God Who Is Present*<br>God said, "I will never leave you nor forsake you" (Hebrews 13:5). Jesus said, "I am with you always, even to the end of the age" (Matthew 28:20). God is not only all around us; His Spirit lives inside of every believer (1 Corinthians 3:16; 6:19). He is with you everywhere you go and in whatever you are going through. | Ezekiel 48:35; Daniel 3:25; Psalm 46; 139:7–11; Matthew 28:20 |

| Name | Meaning & Application | Scriptures |
|---|---|---|
| Jehovah Shalom | *The Lord Is Your Peace*<br>In Judges 6:24, Gideon called God "Jehovah Shalom" or "The Lord Is Peace." The name and word *shalom* in the original Hebrew of the Old Testament carried the meaning of peace, well-being, good health, and prosperity.[3] Genesis 43:27–28 contains the word *shalom* three times with three different meanings: "Then he asked them about their *well-being*, and said, 'Is your father *well*, the old man of whom you spoke? Is he still alive?' And they answered, 'Your servant our father is in *good health*; he is still alive.'"<br>God gives us supernatural peace, well-being, good health, and prosperity. He gives us a peace the Bible says "surpasses all understanding" (Philippians 4:7). That means it is a peace that doesn't even make sense in the midst of adversity. | Genesis 43:27–28; Numbers 6:26; Judges 6:24; Isaiah 9:6 |
| Jehovah Baal Perazim | *The God of the Breakthrough*<br>David called God this name when he was surrounded by enemies and God supernaturally delivered him. He said, "The LORD has broken through my enemies . . . like a breakthrough of water" (2 Samuel 5:20). Keep standing in faith and trusting God. He's the God of the breakthrough, and He is going to break through for you! | 2 Samuel 5:20 |
| Jehovah Rohi | *God Your Shepherd*<br>He cares for you, tends to you, protects you, and provides for you. | Psalm 23:1–3; Isaiah 53:6; John 10:14–18; Hebrews 13:20 |
| Jehovah Jireh | *The Lord Will Provide*<br>God is our Source and our Provider. Our job is not our source. The economy is not our source. God uses those things, but He is our Source. He is not limited to the economy or anything in the natural. The Bible is replete with stories about God providing in supernatural and unusual ways. Often, health challenges can bring financial challenges as well. Trust God to meet all your needs in abundance. Like David wrote in Psalm 23:1, declare over yourself, "The LORD is my shepherd. I lack nothing" (CEB). | Genesis 22:13–14; Psalm 23:1; Mark 10:45; Romans 8:2; Philippians 4:19 |
| Jehovah Nissi | *The Lord Your Banner*<br>As you battle your illness and any other challenge in life, know that God Himself is your banner in the midst of the battle, and that banner is love, healing, victory, peace, and prosperity. | Exodus 17:15–16; Deuteronomy 20:3–4; Isaiah 11:10–12; 2 Corinthians 2:14; 1 John 4:16 |

| Name | Meaning & Application | Scriptures |
|---|---|---|
| Jehovah Sabbaoth | *The Lord of Hosts*<br>God commands the heavenly hosts, the angels. He gives His mighty angels charge over you to keep you in all your ways and bear you up in their hands (Psalm 91:11–12). He dispatches mighty angels to fight for you and minister to you when you need strength and encouragement. Even Jesus needed angels to minister to Him after He was tempted by the devil and when He was grieving in the Garden of Gethsemane (Matthew 4:11; Luke 22:43). | 1 Samuel 1:3; 17:45; 2 Samuel 6:2; 7:26–27; 1 Chronicles 11:9; Haggai 1:5; Psalm 46:7; 91:11–12; Isaiah 6:1–3; Malachi 1:10–14; Matthew 4:11; Luke 22:43 |
| El Elyon | *The Most High God*<br>You may have some big challenges, but God is the Most High God. God is higher, bigger, stronger, and greater than anything you are facing. He's never lost a battle! Don't tell God how big your problems are; tell your problems how big your God is. The bigger you make God in your mind, the smaller your problems will become. | Psalm 78:35; Daniel 4:34 |
| Elohim | *The All-Powerful One; Creator*<br>God has *all* power to heal you, deliver you, provide for you, or do whatever you need Him to do. He spoke the universe into existence, parted the Red Sea, and raised Jesus from the dead after three days. Nothing is impossible with Him! He is way more powerful than any sickness, enemy, adversity, or obstacle you face. | Genesis 1:1–3; Deuteronomy 10:17; Psalm 6:8 |
| El Roi | *The God Who Sees*<br>God sees everything. Nothing we are going through escapes His awareness. The Bible says a sparrow does not fall to the ground without Him knowing about it, and He cares about you so much more than He does a sparrow. He is not a distant, aloof God, but a loving, personal God who sees and cares about everything you are going through and everything you feel. | Genesis 16:11–14; Psalm 139:7–12 |

## Names of Jesus

The most common names for Jesus are "Lord," "Christ" (which means "Anointed One"), and Messiah. The following is a list of other names for Jesus in the Bible. As you read through these names, let them fill your heart with praise and thanksgiving for everything Jesus is in your life. Use these names to praise Him, and incorporate them into your prayers.

| | |
|---|---|
| Rock of my salvation | 2 Samuel 22:47 |
| The light of the morning | 2 Samuel 23:4 |
| The lifter of mine head | Psalm 3:3 |
| My rock | Psalm 18:2 |
| My fortress | Psalm 18:2; 144:2 |
| My deliverer | Psalm 18:2; 144:2 |
| My strength | Psalm 18:2 |
| The horn of my salvation | Psalm 18:2 |
| My stronghold | Psalm 18:2; 144:2 CSB |
| My Shepherd | Psalm 23:1 |
| My goodness | Psalm 144:2 KJV |
| My shield | Psalm 18:2; 144:2 |
| A friend that sticks closer than a brother | Proverbs 18:24 |
| Lord of Hosts | Isaiah 6:3 |
| Wonderful | Isaiah 9:6 |
| Counselor | Isaiah 9:6 |
| Mighty God | Isaiah 9:6 |
| Everlasting Father | Isaiah 9:6 |
| Prince of Peace | Isaiah 9:6 |
| My strength and my song | Isaiah 12:2 |
| A shade from the heat | Isaiah 25:4 |
| A refuge from the storm | Isaiah 25:4 |
| A diadem of beauty | Isaiah 28:5 |
| A sure foundation | Isaiah 28:16 |
| The Holy One of Israel | Isaiah 49:7 |
| The Redeemer | Isaiah 59:20 |
| Balm of Gilead[4] | Jeremiah 8:22 |
| Ancient of Days | Daniel 7:9, 13, 22 |
| A wall of fire | Zechariah 2:5 |
| The Messenger of the covenant | Malachi 3:1 |
| A refiner and purifier of silver | Malachi 3:3 |

| | |
|---|---|
| The Sun of Righteousness | Malachi 4:2 |
| Immanuel | Matthew 1:23 |
| A friend of sinners | Matthew 11:19 |
| The Holy One of God | Mark 1:24 |
| Our brother | Mark 3:35 |
| The Word | John 1:1 |
| The light of men | John 1:4 |
| The Lamb of God | John 1:29 |
| The Christ, the Savior of the world | John 4:42 |
| The Bread of Life | John 6:35 |
| The Light of the World | John 8:12 |
| I AM | John 8:58 |
| The door of the sheep | John 10:7 |
| The Good Shepherd | John 10:11 |
| The resurrection | John 11:25 |
| The way, the truth, and the life | John 14:6 |
| The Vine | John 15:5 |
| God's Holy One | Acts 2:27 |
| Lord of all | Acts 10:36 |
| The firstborn among many brethren | Romans 8:29 |
| The Deliverer | Romans 11:26 |
| The power and wisdom of God | 1 Corinthians 1:24 |
| The foundation | 1 Corinthians 3:11 |
| Our Passover | 1 Corinthians 5:7 |
| A life-giving Spirit | 1 Corinthians 15:45 |
| The image of God | 2 Corinthians 4:4 |
| God's unspeakable gift | 2 Corinthians 9:15 KJV |
| Head over all things | Ephesians 1:22 |
| He who fills all in all | Ephesians 1:23 |
| Our peace | Ephesians 2:14 |
| An offering and sacrifice to God | Ephesians 5:2 |
| The image of the invisible God | Colossians 1:15 |
| Creator of all things | Colossians 1:16 |
| The head of the body | Colossians 1:18 |
| The firstborn from the dead | Colossians 1:18 |
| All in all | Colossians 3:11 |
| Lord of Peace | 2 Thessalonians 3:16 |
| Our Hope | 1 Timothy 1:1 |
| The Mediator | 1 Timothy 2:5 |
| God made manifest in the flesh | 1 Timothy 3:16 |
| Judge of the living and the dead | 2 Timothy 4:1 |

| | |
|---|---|
| The righteous Judge | 2 Timothy 4:8 |
| The brightness of God's glory | Hebrews 1:3 |
| The express image of God's person | Hebrews 1:3 |
| The upholder of all things | Hebrews 1:3 |
| The captain of our salvation | Hebrews 2:10 |
| Our High Priest | Hebrews 3:1 |
| The Great High Priest | Hebrews 4:14 |
| High Priest forever | Hebrews 5:6 |
| Author of eternal salvation | Hebrews 5:9 |
| The forerunner | Hebrews 6:20 |
| Surety of a better covenant | Hebrews 7:22 |
| Our intercessor | Hebrews 7:25 |
| Mediator of a better covenant | Hebrews 8:6 |
| Author and finisher of our faith | Hebrews 12:2 |
| Mediator of the new covenant | Hebrews 12:24 |
| The Lamb without blemish or spot | 1 Peter 1:19 |
| The Bishop (Overseer) of our souls | 1 Peter 2:25 |
| The Chief Shepherd | 1 Peter 5:4 |
| The morning star | 2 Peter 1:19 |
| The Word of Life | 1 John 1:1 |
| The Savior of the world | 1 John 4:14 |
| The firstborn from the dead | Revelation 1:5 |
| The Alpha and Omega | Revelation 1:8 |
| The Almighty | Revelation 1:8 |
| The First and the Last | Revelation 1:17 |
| King of saints | Revelation 15:3 |
| Lord of Lords | Revelation 17:14 |
| King of Kings | Revelation 17:14 |
| Lord God Omnipotent | Revelation 19:6 |
| Word of God | Revelation 19:13 |
| The Bright and the Morning Star | Revelation 22:16 |
| The Lion of the tribe of Judah | Revelation 5:5 |

KEY 6

# Healing the Soul

> Beloved, I wish above all things that you may prosper and be in health, even as your soul prospers.
>
> 3 John 1:2 KJ2000

> If your soul is healthy, no external circumstance can destroy your life.
>
> John Ortberg

YOU ARE GOD'S CHILD. He wants you to be healthy, whole, and victorious in every way. He wants to heal not only your body, but the hurt places in your soul. Going through a serious illness is hard enough without carrying extra baggage around in your soul. You need your soul to be healthy and strong so nothing hinders your physical healing.

The Bible describes the soul as our mind, will, and emotions.[1] It is the place where we harbor hurts and pains, disappointments, bad memories, and the internal damage people and life have inflicted on us. Unhealthiness in our soul affects every area of our lives. It can cause us to think wrong thoughts, have toxic emotions, make flawed decisions, and engage in harmful behaviors. It affects our relationships and overall quality of life. But most relevant to you as you seek physical healing, unhealthiness in your soul can cause sickness and disease in your body and block your healing. Often, people's physical healing will not come until they first get healed in their souls.

Studies show that 75 to 90 percent of physical ailments are connected to negative thoughts and emotions.[2] That is our soul, even though science and medicine don't use that term. In her book *Who Switched Off My Brain?*, Dr. Caroline Leaf writes, "Research shows that around 87 percent of illnesses can be attributed to our thought life, and only 13 percent to diet, genetics, and environment."[3] Every stressful, angry, or negative thought we think has an emotion attached to it, and these toxic thoughts and emotions directly affect our physical health. They create a cascade of electrical and chemical stress responses in our bodies that weaken our immune systems and open the door to disease. In fact, the word *disease* is a compound of the root words *dis* and *ease*, which means "against ease." Disease occurs when we have a lack of ease in our body caused primarily by these soul issues.

The Bible corroborates the fact that good health and healing start in our souls. Third John 2:1 says, "Beloved, I wish above all things that you may prosper and be in health, even *as your soul prospers*" (KJ2000). Notice how this verse connects prospering and being in good health directly with the phrase "as your soul prospers." You can pray till the cows come home and have everybody else praying for you, but many times physical healing won't come until your soul gets healthy and prospers. Healing the soul is often a hidden key to receiving physical healing.

The Bible tells the story of a blind man who was begging on the side of the road when Jesus came to his town. He had heard about Jesus' miracles and had great anticipation as the crowd signaled Jesus was approaching. He cried out, "Jesus, Son of David, have mercy on me!" (Luke 18:38). People told him to be quiet, but he cried out even louder. Jesus stopped and asked the man what seems like an odd question: "What do you want Me to do for you?" (Luke 18:41). Clearly, He could see the man was blind. He could have just healed him and moved on. Why did He ask him such an obvious question? We assume everybody wants to be healed, but that is not always the case.

As a pastor for over twenty years, I have counseled thousands of people and encountered many who don't really want to be healed. They want to keep holding on to the pain in their soul. It has become part of their identity. It has become their normal. They talk about it a lot, but they don't really want to be free from it. They may even like the attention and sympathy they get from it. If we are going to live freely and victoriously, we have to let God heal the hurt places in our souls. Jesus said, "Behold, I stand at the door and knock. If anyone hears My voice and opens the door, I will come in" (Revelation 3:20). Jesus wants to come in and heal us, but we have to open the door and let Him in. He is not going to force Himself on us. I pray that you open the door of your heart and allow Jesus to come in and heal all your hurts, pains, and disappointments. There is no pain God can't heal, except the pain we won't give to Him. The Scripture says He will give us beauty

**There is no pain God can't *heal*, except the pain we won't *give* to Him.**

for ashes, but to receive the beauty, we have to give Him our ashes (Isaiah 61:3). Let go of the past. Let go of the pain and offenses. Let go of unforgiveness, anger, and bitterness. When you get healed on the inside, your physical healing will follow.

There are many types of soul wounds and contaminants, but I want to focus on the three most common I have seen in 25 years of ministering to the sick: unforgiveness, disappointment, and bitterness. Most other soul issues are connected to one of these three, and the principles I share can be applied to other soul issues as well.

## Unforgiveness

All of us have been hurt by other people, including those closest to us. People are flawed, and we say and do things that hurt each other from time to time. Unforgiveness occurs when we hold on to those hurts and they become embedded in our soul. Our sense of justice expects the person who hurt us to pay us back or at least suffer consequences. But that is not how God treated us. There was no way to pay God back for our own sins, so He sent Jesus to pay the price for us on the cross. Because of Jesus' shed blood, God released us from our sins and the eternal punishment we deserved. How can we receive so much grace and forgiveness from God and then refuse to give it to others? Forgiveness means *release*. When we forgive those who hurt us, we release them and our pain to God. We release them from paying us back for what they did to us. The reality is, they can't pay us back. Only God can. And He will only pay us back if we forgive.

The apostle Paul modeled for us how to respond in a mature way when people hurt us. In 2 Timothy 4:14, he said, "Alexander the coppersmith did me much harm. May the

Lord repay him according to his works." Paul was saying, "I'm moving on with my destiny, and I'm going to let God deal with Alexander." Paul knew better than to let other people's actions control or poison him. He wrote, "Beloved, do not avenge yourselves . . . for it is written 'Vengeance is Mine, I will repay,' says the Lord" (Romans 12:19). When you forgive those who have wronged you and release them to God, He promises to deal with them and repay you for the wrong.

Choosing to forgive others not only releases them, *it releases us*. When Jesus raised Lazarus from the dead, he walked out of the tomb but was still bound with graveclothes (John 11:44). That's a picture of us many times. Spiritually, we are born again, but we are still walking around bound by the graveclothes of unforgiveness because of something someone did or said to us years ago. That person has probably gone on with their life and is not even thinking about what they did to us. They may even be dead and gone. Our unforgiveness doesn't affect them one iota; it just makes us miserable and prevents us from living a victorious life. When we forgive, it cuts those graveclothes off and frees us up to live our best lives.

In Mark 11:25, Jesus said, "And whenever you stand praying, if you have anything against anyone, forgive him, that your Father in heaven may also forgive you your trespasses." He was basically saying, "Don't even bother praying if you have unforgiveness in your heart." If you are praying for your healing and harboring unforgiveness, your prayers won't work. In another verse, Jesus said, "If you do not forgive men their trespasses, neither will your Father forgive your trespasses" (Matthew 6:15). God will only forgive us when we forgive others. When we refuse to forgive, we are in a dangerous place because God will not forgive us our trespasses.

That means we are not in right standing with Him and He can't bless us the way He wants to. In fact, *unforgiveness is one of the greatest blessing blockers there is.*

I understand that forgiving others can be very difficult. I'm not telling you to do something I haven't walked through many times myself. Sometimes the pain is so deep it is hard to let go of. We hang on to it like old luggage. We nurse it. We obsess over it. And after a while, we get used to it taking up residence in our soul. If we are not careful, the pain becomes a part of our identity without us even realizing it. We limp through life like a wounded victim. But that is not God's will for us. He wants our soul to be healthy, pure, and free. That's why He commands us to forgive others. In fact, Jesus said we are to forgive "seventy times seven," which means to forgive as many times as we need to (Matthew 18:22). Jesus wasn't saying we should be a doormat and allow people to abuse and mistreat us. There is a place for healthy boundaries and loving certain people from a distance. But we need to forgive them in our hearts. The good news is that God never asks us to do anything He doesn't give us the ability to do. He doesn't expect us to do it alone; He will help us if we ask Him. He will also heal our soul of all the pain if we let Him.

**If you are *praying* for your healing and *harboring* unforgiveness, your prayers won't work.**

Choosing to forgive often leads to sudden, miraculous breakthroughs. Charles and Frances Hunter were a couple at our church who had an amazing worldwide healing ministry for over fifty years before they passed away in their late nineties. Countless people received miraculous healings through their ministry. God showed them that forgiveness was often the lynchpin that led to people's physical healing.

Many times, people had faith to be healed, were receiving much prayer for their healing, and were doing everything else they knew to do, but they had not dealt with unforgiveness toward people who had hurt them. When they ministered to people in this area and led them in a prayer of forgiveness, often their healing came suddenly. They saw this pattern again and again.

I will never forget a visit I had with an elderly cancer patient. When I entered the room, she said there were some things she wanted to get off her chest. I pulled up a chair and sat down, and for the next hour she unloaded years of anger and pain. She told how she had the most wonderful husband for many years, how he was so doting and loving, and how they traveled the world together. Then he got sick, and in her opinion, the doctors who treated him made catastrophic mistakes that led to his demise. She went on and on about those doctors and was seething with anger, even though her husband had been dead for seven years. She even had anger toward her husband for leaving her. Then she shared how her children rarely came to see her, even in the hospital, because they were so selfish and caught up in their own lives.

After an hour of listening, I began to minister to her. I told her I understood that all those things were painful, but harboring unforgiveness was poisoning her life and hindering her healing. I shared some Scriptures and encouraged her to release and forgive all the people who had hurt her and to give the pain to God. God wants to heal our souls, but we have to do our part. She agreed that she would, and I led her in a prayer of forgiveness and release where she named all the people who had hurt her and forgave them. You could feel the atmosphere shift in the room. By the time I left, it felt like a huge weight had been lifted from her. Her whole countenance was better. I followed up and prayed with her weekly, and as her soul was cleansed of all the unforgiveness and anger, God began doing miracles in her battle with cancer.

The Bible tells the story of Job, described as "a blameless and upright man . . . who feared God and shunned evil" (Job 1:1). He had a happy family, great wealth, and a wonderful life. But the devil came against him and attacked every area of his life. His family died, he lost all his possessions, and he suffered from painful boils all over his body (Job 2:7). If that wasn't bad enough, his so-called friends turned on him in his darkest hour. Instead of consoling and encouraging him, they accused him of secretly sinning and claimed God was punishing him. Of course, that wasn't true.

Any of us would understand how Job might be deeply hurt and offended. I imagine he was very tempted to have unforgiveness and bitterness toward them. But instead, Job refused to take the bait of offense. He didn't allow his so-called friends to poison him and damage his soul. Not only did he forgive them, he prayed for them. Because Job kept his heart right, God restored everything back to him, including his health. In fact, God gave Job *twice* as much as he had before and blessed his latter days more than his former days (Job 42:10, 12). That's the power of forgiveness. Give yourself a double blessing like Job and forgive.

If you feel like you have unforgiveness toward anyone, I encourage you to take the following steps to forgiveness:

1. Reflect on how much God has forgiven you.
2. Remember that God loves your offender as much as He loves you.
3. Repent for harboring unforgiveness. Ask God to forgive you, cleanse you, and help you to truly forgive.

4. Decide to permanently release the debt they owe you. Release the punishment, the person, and the pain to God.
5. Bless and pray for the person. This may be really difficult, but you can do it with God's help.
6. Don't rehearse what they did and talk about it.
7. Any time you have a feeling, thought, or memory that brings up the hurt, go through these steps again.

In the "Unlocking Healing with Key 6" section at the end of this chapter, I have included a specific prayer to overcome unforgiveness. I encourage you to pray this prayer as often as you need to if you feel as if you have any unforgiveness in your heart.

## Disappointment

Disappointment is another soul issue I have encountered a lot with those battling illness. Perhaps you feel disappointment about your health situation and its impact on your life. Your identity and roles in life may have dramatically changed from being a parent, spouse, grandparent, sibling, friend, and whatever your career was to being a person with a certain illness. Maybe you had to give up your job. If you are in a hospital, you have lost the privacy and comfort of your home. You may also feel isolated from your family, friends, and church. It is amazing how many people battling a serious illness have told me they feel abandoned by many of their family and friends. People have busy lives, and they may not know how to handle the situation or what to say, so they may rarely call or visit. All of this can add up to painful disappointment in the soul.

Left unchecked, disappointment can harden our hearts and cause us to become negative and discouraged. We can take on a victim spirit and stop expecting good. In fact, we are waiting for the next shoe to drop. The invisible prison of disappointment robs our motivation and joy and neutralizes our faith. It keeps us from believing, hoping, and praying with fervency. We stop exercising our faith, which produces more disappointment, because faith is how we receive anything from God. When it gets to this point, disappointment has gotten lodged in the soul and become a mindset.

This reminds me of what happens to elephants trained for the circus. The trainers start out tying the elephant to a post when it is a baby. The elephant gets so conditioned to being tied to the post that it stops trying to break free. By the time it grows up into a huge, powerful elephant, the trainer can tie it to a stick in the ground, and it won't make the slightest attempt to get away.

That's how disappointment works. People with illness often start out having faith for their healing and for everything to end well. But as time goes on, they can get worn down. Perhaps they aren't seeing any progress, or their condition has worsened, and they keep getting negative reports from the doctor. I have seen too many patients give up and stop believing for their healing when this happens. That's why disappointment is one of the biggest blocks to healing and must be resisted with every fiber of your being.

I am asking you to stir up your faith again. You may have been waiting a long time for your breakthrough, but if you stay in faith and refuse to give up, God can move suddenly. All it takes is one touch from God to turn your situation around.

You may even feel great disappointment with God. When people are battling a serious illness, the enemy loves to tell them God hasn't kept His word, doesn't care about them, and has forgotten or abandoned them. When you agree with those lies, disappointment can cause you to be angry and resentful toward God, and that will create a major wedge in your relationship with Him. Then you feel guilty about your disappointment with God, which makes you feel even more distant from Him. If any of this describes you, I want you to know it is common. It doesn't mean you are a bad Christian. Some of the greatest people in the Bible felt this way. I think most people have. Be encouraged that God doesn't hold it against you. He is big enough to handle it. You may be angry at Him, but He is not angry at you. He loves you unconditionally and understands your feelings. The Bible says Jesus came to the earth as a man and experienced every kind of pain and emotion we have. He even felt abandoned by the Father as He hung on the cross, crying out, "My God, My God, why have You forsaken Me?" (Matthew 27:46; Mark 15:34). The Scripture says, "For we do not have a High Priest who cannot sympathize with our weaknesses, but was in all points tempted as we are, yet without sin" (Hebrews 4:15). Jesus understands and sympathizes with you. He doesn't judge or criticize you. At the same time, He wants you to be free from disappointment. Hanging on to it will keep you stuck where you are and potentially block your healing.

Here are some steps I encourage you to take to break free from disappointment: (1) trust God, (2) refuse to be a victim, and (3) practice thankfulness. Let's look at each of these steps more closely:

**Trust God.** Disappointment usually boils down to unmet expectations. We expected something from our lives, other people, or God that did not happen like we thought it would, and we feel let down. Sometimes we can want something so badly—an unmet need, an expectation, a certain outcome, even a promise of God to manifest in our lives—that it becomes an idol in our lives. It consumes our thoughts. It dominates our prayers. I want to encourage you to let go and trust God. Even when things don't go your way, trust Him. Trust His love for you. Trust His plan. Trust His timing. The Bible says there is an appointed time for everything under the sun. God is not going to be one second late. He does things on His timetable and in His way, not ours. He has the best plans for our lives. He doesn't cause our disappointments, but He uses them to grow us up. Romans 8:28 says He works all things—even our disappointments—together for our good. He wants to forge in us faith and trust that are deeper than our feelings and refuse to be shaken. When you rest in God and trust Him, you are in faith. If you are worried, upset, and frustrated, that is a sign you are not in faith. Release the worry. Release the frustration. Believe that God is in control and will move in your life at the perfect time.

**Refuse to be a victim.** Some people allow their sickness to consume their identity. Being a sick person and a victim becomes their identity and everything their life revolves around. The enemy wants you to feel like a victim. When you accept a victim spirit and self-pity, you are agreeing with the enemy instead of God. You have to refuse to identify as a victim. When God delivered the Israelites from four hundred years of slavery, they left Egypt, but Egypt didn't leave them. God was trying to lead them to the Promised Land, but they still had a victim/slave mentality. They whined, complained, and refused to walk in faith, and they never made it into the Promised Land.

If you are sick, you have to leave your sickness behind in your mind. You can't identify with it. You have to reject it. It is an intruder, a trespasser. It does not belong in your body because your body is the temple of the Holy Spirit, and Jesus already took that sickness upon Himself at the cross two thousand years ago. So don't accept it, yield to it, or learn to live with it. That is the worst thing you can do if you want to be healed. Refuse to have a victim spirit. God says you are a victor and not a victim. Romans 8:37 says in all things you are more than a conqueror. Second Corinthians 2:14 says God always leads you to triumph in Christ. He may not always lead us down the quickest and easiest path, but if we stay in faith, we will prevail in the end.

King David had many devastating disappointments in his life. First Samuel 30 tells the story of David and his men returning home to Ziklag after a battle only to find their homes burned and their wives and children taken away by the enemy. David's men were so devastated and grief-stricken that they wanted to stone him to death. But instead of melting into self-pity, the Bible says David "strengthened himself in the LORD his God" (1 Samuel 30:6). That means he reminded himself how great God is, how He had never let David down before, how He is faithful and trustworthy and a God of restoration. Because David did not give in to disappointment and a victim spirit, God helped him not only defeat the enemy but recover everything that was lost plus extra spoils.

If you will keep the right attitude, stay in faith, and reject a victim mindset, God will pay you back for every unfair thing that has happened to you. He will turn your disappointments around and bring you out with the victory!

**Practice thankfulness.** I covered thankfulness in chapter 5, but I want to touch on it again because it is one of the best antidotes to disappointment. The people I have seen who stayed positive, kept their joy and peace, and received divine healing all had a thankful spirit. They lived with a constant attitude of gratitude. Instead of focusing on your disappointments, for what are you thankful? Train your mind to see the good every day and have a thankful heart. Seeds of disappointment cannot take root in a thankful heart. In the "Unlocking Healing with Key 6" section at the end of this chapter, I have also included a specific prayer to overcome disappointment. I encourage you to pray this prayer if you are struggling with disappointment.

## Bitterness

If we do not deal with unforgiveness, offense, past hurts, and disappointments, they can become supercharged and progress into bitterness, which is especially malignant and dangerous to the soul.

Hebrews 12:15 says, "Looking carefully lest anyone fall short of the grace of God; lest any *root of bitterness* springing up cause trouble, and *by this many become defiled*." To be *defiled* means to be contaminated, led away from the faith, and polluted. When a person has a root of bitterness, it can consume their soul like an aggressive cancer. It spreads to every area of their life. It steals their joy. It twists their mind. Their whole perspective becomes sour and negative. It poisons all their relationships. They can even become suspicious and paranoid. Peter told a man in Acts 8:23, "I see that you are poisoned by bitterness." After a while, bitterness even changes a person's appearance. You can look at their face and body language and see it.

A close member of my family who is now in heaven was a textbook example of someone with a root of bitterness. She battled serious health problems for probably the last thirty years of her life, and I think a lot of it had to do with her bitterness. It had started many decades earlier, when her husband cheated on her. She never forgave him. As she held on to the hurt and offense, it slowly progressed to bitterness.

It was one of the saddest things I ever saw. She was such a charming, sweet, caring lady who loved the Lord, but the bitterness overtook and defiled her in every way. She and her husband were married for 65 years, and much of their marriage was marred by strife, division, anger, and all kinds of foolishness on her part because of her bitterness. She was always angry at somebody, especially him. At times, she went weeks or months without talking to whoever was the latest target of her anger. She became suspicious and paranoid of everyone. She accused her husband of having other affairs. She accused family members and the housekeeper of stealing from her. Bitterness robbed her joy for decades and poisoned everything in her life. In her final years, even her own family couldn't stand to be around her.

Until we deal with the root of bitterness and remove it from our lives, it will continue to bear bad fruit. It's like when there is a bad odor in our refrigerator. Usually it is something hidden in the back that has been there for a while and become spoiled. We can put a box of baking soda in the fridge. We can spray air freshener. But until we find the source of the odor and remove it, our fridge will keep smelling. The way to remove the root of bitterness is to repent, ask God to remove it, and stop feeding it. Forgive people. Release hurts. Let God heal your soul. Live light and free and positive. You only have so much emotional energy, and it takes a lot to be offended and bitter. That's energy you need to battle your illness and get well. The final prayer I have included in the "Unlocking Healing with Key 6" section at the end of this chapter will help you overcome bitterness. Pray this prayer if you need freedom from bitterness, and let God heal your soul.

## UNLOCKING HEALING WITH KEY 6: Prayers to Overcome

### Prayer to Overcome Unforgiveness

*Father, thank You that You never tell us to do anything without giving us the grace and ability to do it. Help me to truly forgive all those who have hurt, wronged, offended, rejected, and betrayed me. Specifically, I choose right now to forgive [name out loud specific people]. I choose to let them off the hook for what they did to me and release them to You. I repent for harboring unforgiveness, bitterness, offense, and anger in my heart toward them or anyone else. I ask You to forgive me and wash me clean of these and other pollutants in my soul. Create in me a clean heart and a pure spirit, O God. Heal and restore my soul as only You can. I pray that my soul would be so healed and restored that it would be like I had never been wounded or damaged. You said, "If anyone is in Christ, he is a new creation; old things have passed away; behold, all things have become new" (2 Corinthians 5:17). Make me that new creation, O God, and let all the old hurts and pains pass away. Help me to have Your kind of love, described in 1 Corinthians 13, which does not take into account a wrong suffered, bears all things, endures all things, hopes all things, and never fails. Remove any stones in my heart from past wounds and help me to love others like I've never been hurt. You commanded us to love our enemies and to pray for and bless those who have persecuted and spitefully used us. So I pray for [name the people you just forgave] and ask You to bless them. I pray all these things in the healing, delivering, restoring name of the Lord Jesus Christ. Amen.*

### Prayer to Overcome Disappointment

*Heavenly Father, I repent for getting into agreement with disappointment and believing the lies of the enemy. I repent for taking on a victim spirit and self-pity. I repent for any disappointment and anger I have had toward You. I ask You to forgive me and deliver me from the grip of disappointment. Help me to be thankful for what I have and what is good in my life instead of focusing on what I don't have and what is not good. According to Philippians 4:8, help my mind to focus only on what is of good report, excellent, and worthy of praise. Renew a steadfast spirit within me, and help me trust You even when I can't trace Your hand or understand what is going on. In Jesus' name, Amen.*

### Prayer to Overcome Bitterness

*Father God, I confess that I have bitterness, anger, and offense in my heart. Thank You that You don't judge me, but You said in 1 John 1:9 that if I confess my sins, You are faithful to forgive and cleanse me of all unrighteousness. Father, I repent for all bitterness, unforgiveness, anger, resentment, and offense in my soul. I ask You to radically deliver me from these things. Pull up bitterness by the root and put it far from me. Heal, cleanse, and restore my soul. Help me to be a pure, godly vessel that Your love and light can flow through. Help me to live light, free, and positive so my body can be healed and I can become all You created me to be. In Jesus' mighty name, Amen.*

7

KEY 7

# Winning the Invisible Battle

> Your adversary the devil prowls around like a roaring lion, seeking whom he may devour.
>
> 1 Peter 5:8

> Whether you believe it or not, you are in a battlefield. You are in warfare.
>
> Pedro Okoro

IN THE BATTLE FOR YOU or your loved one's healing, there is an invisible battle taking place—a spiritual battle with a spiritual enemy. In John 10:10, Jesus describes our spiritual enemy: "The thief does not come except to steal, and to kill, and to destroy." The thief, also known as Satan, the devil, the father of lies, the accuser, and other names in the Bible, is not a Halloween character with a red tail and pitchfork. He is very real, and it is obvious from Jesus' description, he's not playing around. His goal is to steal, kill, and destroy—to wreak havoc in people's lives, especially followers of Christ.

Peter wrote, "Be sober, be vigilant, because your adversary the devil walks about like a roaring lion, seeking whom he may devour" (1 Peter 5:8). Peter tells us very clearly who our adversary is and what his intentions are. One thing is for sure: The devil is not going to roll over and let you waltz out with a miraculous healing that glorifies God and strengthens other people's faith. He is going to fight you for it. If you are going to win the battle for your health, you must know how to win the invisible battle. You can't be passive. You have to dig deep, resist the enemy, and refuse to give up.

After ministering to thousands of sick people for 25 years, I know firsthand how real and intense this invisible battle can be. It can affect your healing and every area of your life. The Bible has much to say about this topic, often referred to as spiritual warfare. You can hardly turn a few pages in the New Testament without reading a story or verse related to spiritual warfare. If God thought it was important enough to address it that much in the Bible, we should pay close attention.

I believe many people have not received their healing and have even died because they lacked the biblical knowledge I share in this chapter. In Hosea 4:6, God said, "My people are destroyed for lack of knowledge." I don't want that to be you. The enemy wants people to stay ignorant. He doesn't want people to learn about him, the way he operates, or the weapons God has given us to defeat him. That's why God took great pains to educate us in the Bible about this topic. Entire Christian books have been written about spiritual warfare, but I am going to give you a crash course on what you need to know as it relates to your healing.

## Origins of the Battle

If you are new to this topic, it is important to understand the origins of spiritual warfare. Before man was created, there was an archangel in heaven named Lucifer. Archangels are the highest-ranking angels, and the Bible only names three: Lucifer was the worship leader in heaven, Michael is the lead warrior who commands the angel armies, and Gabriel is the lead messenger angel.

Lucifer became prideful and wanted to become the object of the worship he led. He thought he could ascend and become higher than God. So he hatched a plan to lead a rebellion against God and somehow persuaded a third of the angels to join him.

> And war broke out in heaven: Michael and his angels fought with the dragon; and the dragon and his angels fought, but they did not prevail, nor was a place found for them in heaven any longer. So the great dragon was cast out, that serpent of old, called the Devil and Satan, who deceives the whole world; *he was cast to the earth, and his angels were cast out with him.*
>
> Revelation 12:7–9

Jesus told His disciples, "I saw Satan fall like lightning from heaven" (Luke 10:18). That's how fast God booted Lucifer and his cohorts out!

After Lucifer was expelled, his name changed to *Satan*, which means "adversary" or "one who opposes," and his angels became dark angels or demons. Notice the above verse says Satan and his demons were cast down to the earth, where you and I happen to live. These dark forces have been at war with God and His angels ever since. When God created Adam and Eve, Satan disguised himself as a snake and persuaded them to sin against God, which led to the fall of man. That's when sin, sickness, and death were introduced into the world.

You and I are still caught in the crossfire between these spiritual forces of good and evil. The apostle Paul wrote, "Put on the full armor of God, so that you can take your stand against the devil's schemes. For our struggle is not against flesh and blood, but against . . . spiritual forces of evil in the heavenly realms" (Ephesians 6:11–12 NIV). The "heavenly realms" Paul refers to in this verse is the spiritual atmosphere around us, where these spirits operate. We are in this battle whether we believe it or not, whether we like it or not, whether we engage or not. Many Christians want to pull the proverbial covers over their heads and pretend the devil doesn't exist, or they think that if they just ignore him he will leave them alone. Unfortunately, that is not the case. The enemy will engage us in battle whether we choose to engage him or not. In the words of Peter, he walks around like a roaring lion, seeking whom he may devour (1 Peter 5:8).

One way the enemy devours people is in their health. The book of Job says, "Satan . . . struck Job with painful boils from the soles of his feet to the top of his head" (Job 2:7). Luke tells the story of a woman who was attacked for eighteen years by a demonic spirit of infirmity (sickness):

> One Sabbath day as Jesus was teaching in a synagogue, he saw a woman who had been *crippled by an evil spirit [other translations say "spirit of infirmity"]*. She had been bent double for eighteen years and was unable to stand up straight. When Jesus saw her, he called her over and said, "Dear woman, you are healed of your sickness!" Then he touched her, and instantly she could stand straight.
>
> Luke 13:10–13 NLT

Notice where this woman's sickness came from. It says an evil spirit of infirmity had attacked her body for eighteen years. There are several stories like this in the Bible. Indeed, *one-third of Jesus' healings involved spiritual warfare*. Acts 10:38 says, "God anointed Jesus of Nazareth with the Holy Spirit and with power, who went about doing good and *healing all who were oppressed by the devil*, for God was with Him." Notice the phrase "healing all who were oppressed by the devil." This verse clearly indicates that many of the people Jesus healed were sick because they were oppressed by the enemy.

I am not suggesting all sickness comes from the enemy, but he can and does attack people's bodies. We never know for sure whether the enemy caused a particular sickness or not, but I tell people to cover all the bases in the battle for their healing. Leave no stone unturned. Even when the enemy is not the direct cause of an illness, he will try to take advantage of it by attacking people's minds with lies, fears, and vexing thoughts. He attacks people with oppression, depression, torment, and many other ways. He will attack any area of our lives if we let him. That is why spiritual warfare is an indispensable part of your healing journey and walking in victory. The good news is: *You are fighting from a position of victory*. God and His angels are on your side. You are equipped to win!

## Submit to God, Resist the Devil

James 4:7 says, "Submit to God. Resist the devil and he will flee from you." The first step in spiritual warfare is to *submit everything to God*. Submit your body, thought life, emotions, will, finances, children, relationships, business/job, everything. Anything that is not totally submitted to God is out from under His covering and vulnerable to the enemy. Say out loud, "Lord, I humble myself before You. I repent for all my sins. I specifically repent for [name any sins you know you need to repent for]. I ask for You to forgive me and cleanse me of all unrighteousness by the blood of Jesus, according to 1 John 1:9. I ask You to close every door to the enemy in my life. I submit my body, thought life, emotions, will, finances, children, relationships, business/job, and everything else in my life to You. I give You a fresh surrender right now and ask Jesus to be the Lord of every area of my life."

The second step in spiritual warfare from the verse above is to *resist the enemy*. Another verse says: "Be sober, be vigilant; because your adversary the devil walks about like a roaring lion, seeking whom he may devour. *Resist him*, steadfast in the faith" (1 Peter 5:8–9). Notice it is up to us to resist the devil. God will help us, but He is not going to resist the enemy for us. We must resist the enemy with the spiritual armor God has given us, the blood of Jesus, and our authority in Christ.

## The Weapons of Our Warfare

God has given us powerful spiritual weapons to resist and defeat the enemy. I've already covered some of the most important weapons in previous chapters—faith, declaring God's Word, prayer, and praise. Paul gives us some valuable information about our spiritual weapons in one of the greatest passages on spiritual warfare:

> Finally, be strong in the Lord and in his mighty power. Put on the full armor of God, so that you can take your stand against the devil's schemes. For our struggle is not against flesh and blood, but against the rulers, against the authorities, against

> the powers of this dark world and against the spiritual forces of evil in the heavenly realms. Therefore put on the full armor of God, so that when the day of evil comes, you may be able to stand your ground, and after you have done everything, to stand. Stand firm then, with the belt of truth buckled around your waist, with the breastplate of righteousness in place, and with your feet fitted with the readiness that comes from the gospel of peace. In addition to all this, take up the shield of faith, with which you can extinguish all the flaming arrows of the evil one. Take the helmet of salvation and the sword of the Spirit, which is the word of God.
>
> Ephesians 6:10–17 NIV

Paul wrote this letter to the Ephesians while sitting in a Roman prison awaiting trial. The Roman soldier's armor provided the perfect metaphor for Paul to describe the spiritual armor God has given us. The passage starts by reminding us to be strong in the Lord and His mighty power. We fight in God's might, not our own. We may be fighting a foe that is stronger than us, but God is much stronger than he is. He is on our side, and He has rigged the battle in our favor!

It goes on to tell us we are not fighting against flesh-and-blood enemies. Our enemy is not people, but spiritual forces of wickedness in "heavenly places." That's the spiritual atmosphere around us where these spirits operate. Paul tells us three times in this passage to "stand" against these spiritual forces. There is nothing passive about the word *stand* in this verse. In the original Greek language, it means to *actively resist* or *fight against*. Paul says, "After you have done everything, stand." That means when we have done everything we know to do—we've prayed, fasted, declared God's Word over ourselves, forgiven everyone—we just need to keep standing. We have to show the enemy we are more determined than he is. If we keep standing, even when we feel like giving up, we will outlast the enemy, and our breakthrough will come.

**We have to *show* the enemy we are more *determined* than he is.**

This passage also instructs us to put on the whole armor of God. We have to put every piece of our armor on, not just a piece or two. God is not going to put it on for us, just like He is not going to put our clothes on us in the morning. It is up to us to put on our full spiritual armor every day. Any piece we neglect to put on leaves us vulnerable. Let's look at each piece of armor and how it relates to healing:

### *Belt of Truth*

Wearing the belt of truth represents studying and knowing the truth of God's Word. Paul mentions this piece of armor first because all the other pieces of the armor depend on you knowing the Word. You have to be steeped in God's Word to use your armor effectively and be a victorious Christian. The Scripture says, "Let the word of Christ dwell in you richly" (Colossians 3:16). Knowing the Word well is essential for defeating the enemy's lies. Deception is one of his favorite weapons. The Bible says he is the father of lies and there is no truth in him (John 8:44). He will lie to you about yourself, your situation, other people, and God. He will accuse you of all your sins and tell you that you're not worthy to receive healing. He will tell you God doesn't love you or care about you. He will do everything he can to talk you out of believing and receiving the promises of God. The best defense against the devil's lies and discouragement is to know God's truth. I encourage you to read or listen to the Word as much as you can every day and try to memorize some key Scriptures like the ones after chapters 2 and 3.

### Helmet of Salvation

The helmet of salvation represents guarding our mind from the enemy. It means we constantly meditate on everything Jesus died to give us—all the benefits of our salvation, including divine health. Ground zero of spiritual warfare is our minds because it is the control center for our lives. Every thought we have, emotion we feel, decision we make, and action we take starts in our mind.

**Ground zero of spiritual warfare is our *minds* because it is the control center for our *lives*.**

The enemy knows if he can control our minds, he can control our lives. He will whisper lies in your mind like "You'll never overcome this illness"; "You're going to die"; "God doesn't care about you"; and "God doesn't hear your prayers." He will try to bombard your mind with fear, discouragement, doubt, and other thoughts contrary to God's Word. He knows if he can get you to meditate on those thoughts, you can't exercise faith for your healing and keep your spirit strong. It is critically important that you guard your mind and keep it going in the right direction. The Scripture says to dwell on whatever is *true*, of *good report*, *excellent*, and *worthy of praise* (Philippians 4:8). Be quick to reject any thought that doesn't fit this description.

The enemy is very sneaky and crafty. He will sneak in and drop thoughts in your mind that are contrary to God's Word. If you meditate on those thoughts, you open the door for the enemy to flood your mind with more defeated thoughts. Before long, you're in a pit of fear, anxiety, and negativity. The enemy will also try to steal your peace, your faith, and your sleep if you let him. You have to wear your helmet of salvation and guard your mind at all times. When negative thoughts come, you can change the channel of your mind just like you change the channels on the TV. Change over to what is positive and true by renewing your mind with God's Word. Read it. Listen to it on audio. Declare Scriptures over yourself, like the ones after chapters 2 and 3. You can also turn on some praise music or listen to a faith-filled message. Be proactive about keeping a positive, victorious mindset. If you fill your mind with the right thoughts, there won't be any room for wrong thoughts.

### *Breastplate of Righteousness*

The breastplate of righteousness represents the righteousness Jesus shed His blood to give us. The Scripture says, "For [God] made [Jesus] who knew no sin to be sin for us, *that we might become the righteousness of God in Him*" (2 Corinthians 5:21). Jesus took all our sins upon Himself and made us the righteousness of God in Him. That means we are perfectly righteous before God and in right standing with Him because of Jesus' sacrifice on the cross. One of the enemy's favorite tricks is to accuse us of our sins and failures, and weigh us down with condemnation, guilt, and shame. The Bible calls him the "accuser of our brethren" (Revelation 12:10). I have seen a lot of people battling illness fall for this lie, and it was a major block to receiving their healing. How can we receive from God if we think we are unworthy because of our past sins? How can we believe that God wants to heal us if we think He is mad at or disappointed in us? You need to know beyond any doubt that Jesus paid for *all* your sins—past, present, and future—and took away your guilt, shame, and condemnation *forever*. Put on your breastplate of righteousness and reject any feelings of unworthiness, guilt, or shame the enemy tries to put on you. When he tries to accuse you, remind him that Jesus' blood washed away all your sins and made you blameless before God.

### Shoes of Peace

One of the main things the enemy tries to steal is our peace. He knows when we are upset and out of our peace that we can't exercise our faith, fight him effectively, or hear from God. On your journey to healing, there will be innumerable opportunities to lose your peace. It may be pain in your body, lack of sleep, negative doctors' reports, or your own thoughts and emotions. The shoes of Roman soldiers had spikes on the bottom that anchored them in place while fighting. You must be like that Roman soldier: Dig your heels in and refuse to be moved out of your peace for any reason. In the words of Joyce Meyer, "Peace is power. No peace, no power." As a believer, God's supernatural peace that surpasses all understanding is available to you. It's a peace that makes no sense in the natural. It is a fruit of the Holy Spirit that lives inside you. You already have it; you just have to choose to walk in it.

I've found the best ways to walk in your shoes of peace is to keep your mind on God and constantly remind yourself that He is on the throne and in control. He is working everything together for your good. Isaiah 26:3 says, "You will keep him in *perfect peace*, whose *mind is stayed on You*, because he trusts in You." When you focus on God rather than your circumstances and trust Him with all your heart, you can have His perfect peace in any situation. If you are out of your peace, it's a sign your mind is on something besides God. Keep your mind stayed on God and His promises.

### Shield of Faith

I covered faith extensively in chapter 2, so I'll only say a few words about it here. Paul wrote, "Above all, taking the shield of faith with which you will be able to quench all the fiery darts of the wicked one" (Ephesians 6:16). A Roman soldier's shield was held out in front of the other pieces of armor as the first line of defense. This verse says our faith is what quenches (extinguishes) all the fiery darts of the enemy. Fiery darts include sickness, lies, fear, worry, anxiety, discouragement, depression, and anything else the enemy tries to throw at you. Your faith is a spiritual shield that extinguishes and protects you from those fiery darts. When you entertain doubt, you lower your shield of faith and are vulnerable to the enemy's attacks. Don't lay down your faith. Take the steps in chapter 2 to keep your faith strong and your shield of faith held up at all times.

### *Sword of the Spirit, Which Is the Word of God*

The last piece of armor Paul mentions is "the sword of the Spirit, which is the word of God" (Ephesians 6:17). All the other pieces of our armor are defensive in nature—they help us defend against the enemy's attacks. The sword is the only piece that is *offensive*. We use the Word of God in an offensive way to strike and repel the enemy. This is what Jesus did when He was tempted by Satan in the wilderness (Matthew 4:1–11). Three times the devil tempted Jesus to believe lies and succumb to him. Each time, Jesus responded by saying, "It is written," quoting a specific Scripture from the Word of God to counter the lie. That is our model for how to respond when the enemy is attacking our mind with lies and torment. We find a Scripture from God's Word that counters the lie and declare it out loud, as discussed in chapter 3.

For example, when the enemy tells you that you're not going to be healed, you say, "Jesus bore my sicknesses and pains upon Himself at the cross and by His stripes I am healed. No weapon formed against me shall prosper" (Isaiah

53:4–5 NIV; Matthew 8:17; 1 Peter 2:24). When he says you're going to die, you say, "I will live and not die to declare the works of the Lord. With long life God will satisfy me" (Psalm 118:17; Psalm 91:16). If he comes against you with fear, you say, "God has not given me a spirit of fear, but of power, love, and a sound mind. There is nothing to fear because the Lord is with me and He will help and deliver me" (2 Timothy 1:7; Isaiah 41:10; Psalm 34:19). For any other problem, you can say, "God is perfecting everything that concerns me. God always causes me to triumph in Christ Jesus. In all things I am more than a conqueror, and I will conquer this, too, with God's help" (Psalm 138:8; 2 Corinthians 2:14; Romans 8:37).

Revelation 12:11 says we overcome the devil with the blood of the Lamb (Jesus) and the *word of our testimony.* The word of our testimony is our declaration of what God's Word says about us. The Word of God is the sword of the Spirit. When you declare God's Word, it's like a sword coming out of your mouth that thrashes and defeats the enemy. Just like Jesus in the wilderness, when you keep declaring the Word, you will repel the enemy's attacks, and he will leave you alone.

## The Blood of Jesus

Another incredibly powerful protectant we have against the enemy's attacks is the blood of Jesus. When God delivered the Israelites from slavery in Egypt, the last plague He sent was the death of all the firstborn in the land. He told Moses to have each Israelite family sacrifice an unblemished lamb and put its blood on the doorpost of their house. When the death angel saw the blood on the doorpost, he knew to pass over that home and not kill the firstborn child inside. The blood protected God's people.

That Passover lamb was a foreshadowing of Jesus, the perfect Lamb of God, whose blood would be shed for our sins many years later. The Bible calls Him our Passover Lamb (1 Corinthians 5:7). Revelation 12:11says we overcome the devil with the *blood of the Lamb (Jesus)* and the word of our testimony. We overcome the enemy with the blood of Jesus. When we spiritually apply His blood to ourselves, our family, our finances, and other areas of life, it repels the enemy like the blood on the Israelites' doors repelled the death angel. I encourage you to use this powerful weapon against the enemy by saying out loud every day, "I apply the blood of Jesus to every cell in my body, my mind, my home (or hospital room), my family, and [name anything else you want to apply the blood to]. Devil, you cannot cross the bloodline. I overcome you with the blood of the Lamb." I personally do this every day.

## Your Authority in Christ

Lastly, I want to talk about your authority in Christ over the enemy. In Luke 10:19, He said, "Behold, *I give you* the authority to trample on serpents and scorpions, and *over all the power of the enemy*." Serpents and scorpions symbolize the enemy in this verse. Jesus gave you the authority to *trample* on the enemy and over *all* his power! *Trample* is not a soft, passive, demure word. It means "to stomp on and crush." That's what Jesus gave you authority to do to the enemy when he attacks you.

He also gave you authority over *all* the enemy's power. Your authority in Christ is your trump card in spiritual warfare. In Luke 10:17, when the seventy believers Jesus sent out returned, they said, "*Lord, even the demons are subject to us in Your name*." Because of our authority in Christ, the enemy is subject to us in His name. When we use the name of Jesus, the forces of darkness must submit to us. In Mark 16:17, Jesus said, "And these signs will follow those who believe: In My name they will cast out demons. . . ." Jesus said anyone who believes in Him would be able to cast out demons or command them to go. He gave this authority to all believers, not just pastors, priests, and religious professionals. Jesus and His disciples, who are our role models, never prayed demonic spirits away. They used their authority and *commanded* them to go. We don't pray and ask God to get the devil off our backs. He gave us authority over the enemy, and He expects us to use it.

Authority does no good unless it is used. A policeman has authority to stand in the middle of a busy street and stop traffic. He simply raises his hand, and large vehicles that could flatten him have to stop. But if he stands in the street with his hands in his pockets and refuses to use his authority, he's likely to get hurt. In the same way, you have to *use* the authority Christ has given you over the enemy. If you don't walk in your spiritual authority, all that I've just told you about our spiritual weapons and resisting the enemy won't do much good because the enemy will take advantage of you. When the enemy attacks your body with sickness, your mind, your finances, or any area of your life, you must use your authority and *command* him to go. If you have children, talk to the enemy like you do to your children when they get on your last nerve. If you are new to this topic, below are some suggestions for what to say to exercise your authority over the enemy:

- "I bind, cut off, cancel, and nullify every demonic assignment and attack against me, in Jesus' name."
- "I command every attack against my body and health to cease, in the name of Jesus."

- "I bind, rebuke, and cast out every spirit of infirmity, death, destruction, fear, hopelessness, depression, discouragement, torment, or any other demonic spirit from me and from my room/house, in Jesus' name."
- "I cast down every lie, wrong belief, and fearful imagination from my mind, in Jesus' name."
- "I command the enemy to leave my body, leave my mind, leave my house/room, leave my sleep, leave my finances, leave my family, leave every area of my life, in the name of Jesus!"

## UNLOCKING HEALING WITH KEY 7: Spiritual Warfare Prayer

*Father God, Your Word says in James 4:7, "Submit to God. Resist the devil and he will flee from you." I humble myself before You today and repent for all my sins. I specifically repent for [name any sins you know you need to repent for]. I ask You to forgive me and cleanse me of all unrighteousness by the blood of Jesus, according to 1 John 1:9. I ask You to close every door to the enemy in my life. I submit my body, thought life, emotions, will, finances, children, relationships, business/job, and everything else in my life to You. I give You a fresh surrender right now and ask Jesus to be the Lord of every area of my life.*

*Thank You, Lord, that You have given me supernatural weapons and armor to resist the enemy, and Your Word says when I resist him, he will flee from me. So I put on the whole armor of God and take my stand against the enemy. I declare that the weapons of my warfare are not carnal but mighty in God. Thank You, Lord, that I am resisting the enemy from a position of victory. I am positioned with Christ above all demonic powers (Ephesians 1:20–22; 2:6). The devil and his demons are under my feet and subject to me in Your name (Luke 10:17). Luke 10:19 says You have given me authority to trample on snakes and scorpions and over all the power of the enemy. So I trample on every demonic spirit attacking me right now, in the mighty name of Jesus. I bind, cut off, cancel, and nullify every demonic assignment and attack against my body, mind, and every area of my life, in the name of Jesus. I command every demonic spirit to leave me and every area of my life, and to not come back, in Jesus's mighty name. Lord, Your Word says we overcome the devil with the blood of the Lamb and the word of our testimony (Revelation 12:11). So in the name of Jesus I cover every cell in my body with the healing, delivering, restoring blood of Jesus. I cover my mind with the blood of Jesus and cast down lies, fear, discouragement, and every vexing thought, in Jesus' name. I cover my room with the blood of Jesus and command every demonic spirit to leave my room, in Jesus' name.*

*Father, Your Word says You have given Your angels charge over me to keep me in all my ways and bear me up in their hands (Psalm 91:11). Surround me with Your mighty warring and defending angels to do battle for me in the spirit realm. Put Your hedge of protection around me on all sides so that the enemy cannot penetrate (Job 1:10). Thank You that You are my strong tower, my shield and buckler, my refuge and fortress, and my sure defense. In You I dwell in safety and security. I am more than a conqueror through Christ who loves me. No weapon formed against me shall prosper. God always causes me to triumph in Christ Jesus. I will triumph over every attack of the enemy and over this sickness, in Jesus' name! It's in the name above all names—the matchless, all-powerful name of Jesus—that I pray all these things, Amen.*

KEY 8

# Taking Care of Your Temple

> Your body is the temple of the Holy Spirit . . . glorify God in your body.
>
> 1 Corinthians 6:19–20

> I believe that the greatest gift you can give your family and the world is a healthy you.
>
> Joyce Meyer

IN THE INTRODUCTION, I said that faith has two parts: our part and God's part. God will not fail to do His part, but He expects us to do our part. He has given us one body to last us a lifetime, and He expects us to be a good steward of it. So many illnesses are caused, at least in part, by people not taking care of their bodies. We can do all the previous seven keys to healing, but if we get this key wrong, it may all be for naught. The body has an incredible ability to heal itself through proper nutrition, exercise, and other healthy lifestyle choices, but it is up to us to make those choices. In this chapter, I want to educate, equip, and inspire you to make healthy choices that will help you heal and feel your best.

For over a decade, I have been studying nutrition and wellness and educating others about it. I have a Facebook group called *Healthy You* with thousands of members, where we share the latest information on nutrition and fitness and healthy recipes. I don't claim to be a health expert, just a health enthusiast and advocate. I want to share with you some great information I have learned about how to overcome and prevent disease. If you are battling cancer, I also recommend the book *Chris Beat Cancer*, an incredible resource for beating cancer through a healthy diet and lifestyle.[1]

As I have ministered to thousands of hospital patients over 25 years, I have been horrified by the food and beverages routinely given to patients. White bread, white rice, and mashed potatoes; limp, lifeless canned vegetables with all the nutrients cooked out of them; sugary desserts; and canned sodas. Eating food like this deprives your body of the vital nutrients and energy it needs to fight illness and heal. Cole Kazdin, a four-time Emmy award–winning television journalist who has written for the *New York Times* and other top publications, wrote, "Most hospitals and healthcare facilities in the U.S. have contracts with behemoth industrial food corporations like Aramark, which also provide food service to prisons."[2] An insightful article by Jane Hurst adds,

> When it comes to food, the budget is lacking in most hospitals. They have invested in many other aspects, but not food. The hospital provides a basic low-grade meal that fits their budgetary constraints. Many hospitals use food vendors that

> provide cheap junk food. Most hospital food is processed and has excess sugar. Most meals contain some sort of processed meat, artificially sweetened foods, and sweetened drinks. Some of these foods have been linked to certain cancers. They can create more problems for you and negatively impact or delay your recovery.[3]

Trying to eat healthy in a hospital can be daunting, but where there is a will, there is a way, as the saying goes. You can eat healthy in a hospital if you have the will to, but there is no sugarcoating it: You must be very determined and intentional about it. Think about it as though your life depends on it, because it very well might. Below are some tips to help you eat healthier in the hospital:

**1. Request more vegetables and fresh fruit.** Request that the kitchen not overcook your vegetables, as this severely depletes their nutrient content. You can also request raw vegetables, which are the best nutritionally, like salad or cut-up carrots or cucumbers. Minimize starchy vegetables like corn and potatoes, which readily turn into sugar in the body. The healthiest vegetables to request are spinach, carrots, Brussels sprouts, kale, green peas, asparagus, cabbage, sweet potatoes, collard greens, and green beans. Avoid fruit cups, which are usually swimming in sugary syrup, and request fresh fruit instead. If available, blueberries, strawberries, and blackberries are low-glycemic, loaded with antioxidants, and are a very healthy choice.

**2. Choose fish, chicken, or turkey instead of beef.** These are leaner, healthier options.

**3. Avoid sauces.** These usually contain large amounts of gluten, sodium, sugar, and carbohydrates.

**4. Avoid desserts.** They are loaded with sugar and have no nutritional value.

**5. Avoid fruit juices.** They are loaded with sugar, contain a negligible amount of actual fruit juice, and have almost no nutritional value.

**6. Avoid bread.** Gluten, the protein in wheat that is found in most bread, is one of the most inflammatory foods. Also, bread readily turns into sugar in your body. This applies to both wheat and white bread. One piece of whole wheat bread increases your blood sugar as much or more than table sugar (glycemic index of 72 versus 59 for sugar)! The glycemic index measures how a food item affects your blood glucose. Two pieces of wheat bread have a higher glycemic index than a Snickers bar and raise your blood sugar more than two tablespoons of sugar!

**7. Avoid all sodas, even diet. Drink water instead.** Sodas are liquid poison. The sugary ones spike your blood sugar and contain harmful additives. The diet ones change the bacteria in your gut to produce inflammatory proteins that cause an increase in blood sugar (yes, even though they say zero sugar or calories), insulin resistance, damage to your arteries, and weight gain. So they are anything but "diet." The artificial chemical sweeteners increase your risk of cancer. Diet sodas also triple your risk of stroke or dementia.[4]

**8. Ask family and friends to bring you healthy meals and snacks.**

**9. Order healthy meals from the outside for delivery.** With the ubiquity of companies like Door Dash and Uber Eats, and restaurants that deliver, this is a viable option in most cities.

## Foods to Add or Subtract from Your Diet

By far, the most important part of taking care of our temple is our *diet*. What we put in our mouths is the single greatest determiner of our health. Our daily dietary choices are either fostering health or making us vulnerable to disease. When it comes to proper nutrition, there is no substitute for educating yourself so you can make well-informed nutritional decisions. Hosea 4:6 says, "My people are destroyed for lack of knowledge." I don't want that to be you, so I am going to give you the straight scoop about some foods you should consume more of and some you should avoid so you can win the battle for your health.

### *Five Foods to Eat More Often*

**1. Vegetables and fruits.** Eating more vegetables and fruits is possibly *the* most effective step you can take to improve and protect your health. We should eat five to nine servings of vegetables and fruit daily (in most cases, a serving equals a cup). Less than 10 percent of Americans eat this amount of vegetables and fruits, and one in four Americans eats fewer than one serving a day! Couple this with the fact that a staggering 90 percent of foods Americans consume are processed foods,[5] and it's no wonder we have so much chronic disease in our country. To help your body heal and maintain optimal health, I encourage you to eat a diet that is roughly 80 percent plant-based and 20 percent clean meats and fish. Try to limit snacking to plant-based foods (veggies, fruits, nuts, seeds, and healthy grains).

The benefits of consuming more vegetables and fruits are well-established in clinical studies. A meta study published in the *Journal of Epidemiology & Community Health*, which studied 65,000 people over a seven-year period, concluded that "people who ate the most fruits and vegetables were 33% less likely to die from any cause, compared with people who ate very little of these healthy foods. Their risk of cancer death was 25% lower, and cardiovascular disease fell by

31%."[6] In short, eating more vegetables and fruits yields amazing health benefits and dramatically increases longevity.

Although fruits are a healthy choice, vegetables provide even better disease-prevention power, so try to consume more vegetables than fruits. A study in England conducted on 65,000 people over a twelve-year period found that "vegetables seemed to have a stronger health benefit than fruit. The University College, London researchers found that each daily portion of fresh vegetables consumed reduced the overall death risk by nearly 16% compared to just 4% per portion of fresh fruit."[7]

One last tip on consuming vegetables and fruits: Try to "eat the rainbow." This means eating a variety of different colors. Fruits and vegetables contain powerful phytonutrients that help prevent disease and keep the body healthy and vibrant. Each color of fruits and vegetables represents different phytonutrients. Eating the rainbow helps you get the full range of these disease-fighting phytonutrients.

**2. Berries.** Berries are one of the best foods you can consume. They are rich in antioxidants, low-glycemic so they won't spike blood sugar, anti-inflammatory, and high in fiber, which helps with weight loss and lowering cholesterol and blood pressure.

**3. Healthy fats.** Consuming plenty of healthy fats is essential for good health. Our brains are around 60 percent fat, the myelin sheath that covers our nerves is 80 percent fat, and every cell in our body is covered by a fatty membrane. All of these need to be replenished with fat to function properly. Healthy fats are a much cleaner source of fuel for your body and brain than the typical source of fuel, glucose. In addition, healthy fats boost your metabolism, helping you lose weight; lower low-density (bad) cholesterol; raise high-density (good) cholesterol; and lower overall cholesterol.

Good sources of healthy fats are nuts (especially almonds, pecans, macadamia, pistachios, and walnuts); avocados; extra-virgin olive oil; MCT oil; and wild-caught "oily fish" like Alaskan salmon, sardines, and mackerel.

The healthiest oils to cook with are (1) extra-virgin olive oil, (2) avocado oil, (3) coconut oil, (4) grass-fed butter or ghee, and (5) macadamia nut oil.

**4. Clean meats.** Eat organic grass-fed beef, natural chicken, and other meats that do not contain hormones or antibiotics and were fed a non-GMO diet.

**5. Wild fish.** The healthiest fish to eat are wild SMASH fish:

S—Salmon

M—Mackerel

A—Anchovies

S—Sardines

H—Herring

These fish are the cleanest and have the highest omega-3 content. Avoid all farm-raised fish, tilapia, catfish, and tuna (because of its mercury content).

### *Six Foods to Avoid*

**1. Sugar and bad carbohydrates.** From all the research I've done on health and wellness for over a decade, sugar and bad carbs may be the number-one enemy of good health. Bad carbs are foods that readily turn into sugar in our bodies. Some of the most common examples are breads, cakes, cookies, white rice, white potatoes, corn, almost all breakfast cereals (yes, even the ones that look healthy), prepackaged juices, and sweetened yogurts. Here are some of the many reasons you should avoid sugar and bad carbs like the plague in your diet:

- Sugar ravages our body and wreaks havoc on our health.
- Cancer cells love sugar and thrive on it.
- Sugar causes your liver to produce more cholesterol and triglycerides, which clog your arteries.
- Sugar creates a cycle of demand for more sugar, which raises insulin levels, which signals the body to store fat. This makes you gain and retain weight despite other efforts to lose weight.
- Too much sugar overworks your pancreas, causing insulin resistance. If left unresolved, this can lead to prediabetes and type 2 diabetes. This condition is an epidemic in our society, affecting one in two adults, with many not realizing they have it.
- Sugar can depress your immune system by 50 percent for several hours.
- Sugar is inflammatory, and inflammation lies at the root of every chronic disease.
- Sugar is destructive to the gut (intestines). Hippocrates, the father of Western medicine, said, "All disease begins in the gut." Sugar feeds the bad gut bacteria and causes an unhealthy microbiome (the ecosystem of trillions of bacteria that live in your gut). Too much sugar can also cause leaky gut syndrome, a condition where there are holes in the gut that can lead to many health issues.

The food industry uses about twenty different names for sugar on food labels in an effort to hide it. Try to remember these names so you can recognize hidden sources of sugar on labels. Here is a list of common pseudonyms for sugar:

- anything ending in *-ose*, like sucrose, dextrose, glucose, and fructose
- high-fructose corn syrup
- corn syrup
- corn sweeteners
- evaporated cane juice
- malt
- malt syrup
- barley malt syrup
- barley malt extract
- maltodextrin
- brown rice syrup
- maple syrup
- beet juice
- molasses
- honey
- turbinado
- agave

The healthiest sugar substitutes are stevia and monk fruit.

**2. Bad fats.** Avoid hydrogenated and partially hydrogenated fats and animal-based saturated fats. (Coconut oil is 80 to 90 percent saturated fat, but it is a healthy, plant-based saturated fat.) Avoid margarine (especially in stick form) and butter-like spreads, even ones that sound healthy. Eat grass-fed butter or ghee instead. Ghee is simply clarified butter that has been slightly caramelized and had most of the water removed. It is shelf-stable and has a high smoke point, so it is great for cooking. Avoid canola, vegetable, sunflower, grapeseed, corn, soybean, and safflower oils. These oils are highly inflammatory in the body and contain too many omega-6 fats, which Americans already get way too much of.

**3. Gluten.** Gluten is a protein found mainly in wheat-based products. Breads, cookies, cakes, pizza, pasta, and cereals are obvious sources, but there are many hidden sources of gluten. Going gluten-free is not just the latest health fad; there is now a mountain of evidence showing gluten's damaging effects on our health. It is one of the most inflammatory foods you can put in your body, even if you don't think you are sensitive to it. Gluten is also very damaging to our intestines and can cause leaky gut syndrome. It also causes autoimmune responses, weight gain, brain fog, and a host of other negative responses in the body.

**4. Fried foods, fast foods, processed/prepackaged foods like frozen meals and canned foods.** These foods are loaded with unhealthy fats that cause inflammation and clog your arteries. They also contain high amounts of sodium, sugar, and chemical additives, and they have almost no nutritional value. In most cases, you pay for convenience.

**5. Junk food.** Chips, cookies, cakes, pies, candies, ice cream . . . These so-called foods are just dead calories with no nutritional value. Worse, they are loaded with health-damaging ingredients like sugar, gluten, high-fructose corn syrup, and unhealthy fats. They are also highly inflammatory.

**6. Artificial sweeteners and diet sodas.** All artificial sweeteners are bad and increase your risk of cancer, stroke, heart attack, obesity, diabetes, and leaky gut syndrome. Even though they say "zero calories," they change the bacteria in your gut to produce inflammatory proteins that cause an increase in blood sugar, insulin resistance that can lead to obesity and type 2 diabetes, and damage to your arteries. Avoid them like the plague and instead choose natural sweeteners like stevia and monk fruit.

## Guide to Healthy Grocery Shopping

Mark Hyman, MD, director of functional medicine at the prestigious Cleveland Clinic, an eleven-time *New York Times* bestselling author, and one of the top natural medicine doctors in the world, said, "What you put at the end of your fork is more powerful medicine than anything you will find in a pill bottle. Food is the most powerful medicine available to heal chronic disease. All you need to do is eat your medicine and *think of your grocery store as your pharmacy*."[8] I love this quote and believe it wholeheartedly.

The challenge is that there is a dizzying array of choices among the 47,000 products in the average grocery store. The vast majority of those products are "frankenfoods" loaded with dangerous chemicals, sugar, sodium, and other additives and cleverly marketed to make you think they are healthy. Understand that in general the food industry's main priority is *not* your health but making money. *Food is big business.* Americans spend more than half a trillion dollars a year on groceries. The goal of most conventional food companies is to produce food as cheaply and quickly as possible and lure you into buying their products, even if it means using blatant deception. Grocery shopping for optimal health can be like the movie *The Hunger Games*, and the odds are definitely not ever in our favor. That's why we must be educated, know how to read labels, and make wise choices.

In Deuteronomy 30:19, God said, "I have set before you life and death . . . choose life." That is the mindset you need to have when you go to the grocery store or a restaurant. *Choose life.* You only have one body to last a lifetime. You don't get to trade it in for a new one every few years like a car. So give your body the best nutrition you can to heal and stay healthy.

Here are a few general guidelines for healthy grocery shopping:

**Stay on the perimeter.** The healthy, living foods you need to eat for optimal health are mostly found on the perimeter of the grocery store, not the center aisles. The perimeter includes organic produce, fish, healthy meats, eggs, etc.

**Focus on foods that don't need a label.** In other words, produce, meats, seafood, etc. If you have to go down one of the center aisles and buy a product with a label, go for those that have five or fewer natural ingredients that you recognize (i.e., no chemical names or ingredients you can't pronounce). If you don't recognize it, neither will your body!

**Go early.** To the extent you can, avoid times when grocery stores are typically jammed with people. Going early in the morning before the crowd will ensure you get the freshest and best choices of produce and other healthy foods.

**Buy organic.** Pesticides cannot be completely washed off and penetrate into the cellular structure of produce. These pesticides cause cancer, disrupt hormones, and have other negative effects on our body. The little bit extra you pay for organic is well worth it because your health is priceless.

**Buy the produce with the most vibrant colors and that is crisp and fresh.** This will ensure you get vegetables and fruits with the highest nutritional value.

**Focus on foods that will rot.** Avoid packaged and processed foods that can last in your pantry for weeks or months. These are dead, processed foods, rather than living, whole foods. Foods that will rot are living foods that promote good health.

**Buy only plant-based snacks.** These include veggies, fruits, nuts, seeds, healthy grains.

**Avoid foods with sugar grams in the double digits or that contain artificial sweeteners.**

Now we are going to get down to the nitty gritty. I am going to walk you through how to make the healthiest choices in the grocery store with the following alphabetical grocery shopping guide. Remember: Every food choice you make is either moving you toward healing or potentially hindering your healing.

**Artificial sweeteners:** Avoid all artificial sweeteners and foods containing them. The healthiest natural sweeteners are stevia and monk fruit.

**Beef:** Choose grass-fed, organic beef that says it is free from hormones and antibiotics.

**Bread:** Choose gluten-free or sprouted grain varieties (like Ezekiel bread). Avoid white and whole wheat bread. The effect on your blood sugar of eating two pieces of whole wheat bread is the same as eating two tablespoons of sugar!

**Breakfast bars:** I recommend avoiding store-bought breakfast bars altogether. It is impossible to find one that is nutritionally sound. If a "grab and go" option is important to you for breakfast, you can easily make your own breakfast bars using healthy ingredients like seeds, nuts, dark chocolate nibs, and dates. Just Google "healthy breakfast bar recipe," and you'll find some great, easy recipes. Or just eat a piece of fruit or some nuts.

**Breakfast cereals:** I recommend avoiding most breakfast cereals, including those that try to market themselves as "healthy." If you really want cereal, choose one that is grain free (i.e., contains only nuts, seeds, and a few other healthy ingredients) and low in sugar. One of my favorites is a Keto grain-free granola I buy from Costco that only has nuts, seeds, dried blueberries, and cinnamon, and it is sweetened with stevia and monk fruit. It only contains two grams of sugar per serving and zero added sugar. That's an example of the kind of cereal you should look for.

**Butter:** Choose grass-fed, organic butter, like Kerrygold Irish butter or Kirkland (Costco) brand grass-fed butter from New Zealand. Challenge butter is not grass-fed, but it would be the next best choice. Avoid any kind of margarines or butter-like spreads, even ones that sound healthy.

**Cheese:** The healthiest cheeses are feta, Parmesan, and organic sheep or goat cheese. Otherwise, I would avoid or at least minimize cheese for the reasons I state below about milk.

**Chicken:** Choose chicken labeled "natural" or "organic" that specifically says it is free from hormones and antibiotics and is fed a non-GMO diet.

**Coffee:** Organic, non-flavored coffee is the healthiest choice.

**Coffee creamers:** Almost all coffee creamers are unhealthy concoctions, including those that are unsweetened. If you look at their ingredients, you will find a litany of unhealthy ingredients, including corn syrup, inflammatory oils, carrageenan (an additive that is inflammatory), maltodextrin (a thickener that turns into sugar in the body), and others. Choose a natural creamer that is preferably non-dairy (i.e., made from coconut milk, almond milk, etc.) and contains no sugar or unhealthy ingredients.

**Condiments:** Mayonnaise: Avocado mayonnaise is the healthiest option. It is creamy, delicious, and does not taste like avocados. Ketchup: Choose only an organic one with minimal sugar and no high-fructose corn syrup. Mustards: Most are fine as long as they don't contain soybean oil or other additives.

**Cooking oils:** The healthiest oils are extra-virgin olive oil, avocado oil, coconut oil, ghee or grass-fed butter, or macadamia nut oil. Avoid vegetable, canola, corn, sunflower, safflower, soybean, grapeseed, and peanut oils.

**Corn:** Nearly 95 percent of corn in America is genetically modified, so it is best to avoid corn and corn products. Even if you buy organic, it's still a starchy vegetable that spikes blood sugar, so I would eat only small portions.

**Eggs:** The healthiest choice is organic, pasture-raised eggs. The second healthiest are organic and free range. The third healthiest are organic and cage free. I would avoid conventional eggs altogether, as the hens are injected with antibiotics and hormones and fed a GMO grain diet, making their eggs decidedly less healthy than the aforementioned varieties.

**Fish:** See "Seafood," below.

**Honey:** Choose raw, unfiltered honey and eat in moderation, as it will spike your blood sugar.

**Jelly:** Avoid most jellies, as they contain too much sugar. My favorite brand is Nature's Hollow HealthSmart jelly. It is sugar free, delicious, and healthy.

**Kefir:** Kefir is touted as healthy because of the probiotics it contains, but I recommend avoiding it because of the comments under "Milk," below. I strongly recommend taking a daily probiotic with at least thirty billion units and twelve strains of probiotic bacteria. This will provide you immensely more and better probiotics than kefir. If you are set on consuming kefir, plain, unsweetened organic goat milk kefir is the healthiest. Plain, unsweetened kefir made from grass-fed organic cow's milk is also fine. Avoid flavored kefirs, as they are too high in sugar.

**Milk:** I recommend avoiding cow's milk altogether. Mark Hyman, MD, said this about it in his book *Food: What the Heck Should I Eat?*:

> Dairy is nature's perfect food, but only if you are a calf. It does not promote healthy bones or prevent fractures. Milk has more than sixty naturally occurring hormones that can cause cancer and weight gain. And low-fat milk is even worse. . . . [Today's cows' milk contains] allergenic proteins, antibiotics, and growth factors, some of which are known to promote cancer, such as IGF-1 (insulin-like growth factor).

> . . . In fact, studies show that milk may actually make bones weaker. On top of that, there are plenty of better, richer, healthier sources of calcium in food.[9]

A much healthier option than cow's milk is nut milk. My favorite varieties are macadamia nut, walnut, almond, and coconut milks. Go for the ones that are unsweetened and carrageenan-free.

**Nut butters:** Avoid most commercial brands of peanut butter, as they contain unhealthy oils and added sugar. Instead, grind your own peanut or almond butter (almond is healthier) if your grocery store has a grinding machine. If not, buy natural peanut or almond butter with no other ingredients but the ground nuts. My personal favorite is called Nutzo Mixed Nut and Seed Butter. I buy it from Costco, but you can also get it online and from Amazon. The only ingredients are cashews, almonds, Brazil nuts, hazelnuts, flax seeds, chia seeds, pumpkin seeds, and Celtic sea salt.

**Pasta:** Avoid the typical semolina or whole wheat pastas. The heathiest option is spaghetti squash pasta, which is super easy to make. Simply cut a squash in two, scoop out the middle part, and microwave the halves upside down in an inch of water for about twelve minutes or to desired tenderness, then shred it with a fork and scoop out onto your plate. Zucchini pasta is also healthy. You can either buy it premade or purchase zucchini and make it into pasta using a spiral veggie cutter. If you buy packaged pasta, choose those that are gluten-free, especially ones made from quinoa or other ancient grains.

**Produce:** Buy organic to the extent that you can afford it, especially for the "dirty dozen" list of produce most contaminated with pesticides (see below). Understand that you cannot wash off all pesticides, and often they have been absorbed into the main body of the vegetable or fruit. Consuming pesticides can cause cancer, disrupt our hormones, and cause other health problems. "Almost 70 percent of non-organic produce sampled tested positive for pesticide contamination. More than 90 percent of samples of strawberries, apples, cherries, spinach, nectarines, and kale tested positive for residues of two or more pesticides. Kale samples detected 18 different pesticides."[10] The 2022 dirty dozen list for most-contaminated produce is as follows: (1) strawberries, (2) spinach, (3) kale, collard, and mustard greens, (4) nectarines, (5) apples, (6) grapes, (7) cherries, (8) peaches, (9) pears, (10) bell and hot peppers, (11) celery, and (12) tomatoes.[11] This list gets updated annually, but it is pretty much the same twelve culprits every year.

When choosing produce, remember to "eat the rainbow." Choose a variety of different colors because each represents different beneficial phytonutrients. Try to eat a lot of dark, leafy greens and cruciferous vegetables (broccoli, cauliflower, Brussels sprouts). Also, choose produce that has vibrant color and crispness, as these are the freshest and have retained more of their nutrients.

**Protein bars:** Bars are so tempting because of their convenience factor, but most protein and "health" bars are fraught with bad ingredients masked by marketing hype. Avoid those that have any of the following ingredients: (1) soy protein, (2) soy lecithin, (3) sugar in the double digits, (4) artificial sweeteners like sucralose, (5) high-fructose corn syrup, or (6) palm kernel oil. Look for bars that have whey protein isolate (the best non-vegan protein), whey protein or a good vegan protein like pea protein, and no more than two to three grams of sugar.

**Rice:** Choose black, wild, or brown rice. Avoid white rice.

**Salad dressings:** Most salad dressings contain unhealthy oils like canola or soybean, sugar, hidden gluten, and other unhealthy ingredients. The best option is to make your own at home. Otherwise, Walden Farms and Sugar Free Maple Grove Farms salad dressings are healthy options.

**Seafood:** Choose wild Alaskan salmon, albacore tuna (troll or pole-caught in the United States or British Columbia), mackerel, trout, snapper, and wild canned sardines. Avoid all farm-raised fish, particularly tilapia, catfish, shrimp, and salmon.

**Yogurt:** Yogurt is touted as healthy because of the few probiotics it contains, but I recommend avoiding dairy-based yogurt because of the comments under "Milk," above, and because most yogurt is loaded with sugar and has very little probiotic value. If probiotics are what you're after, a much better choice is to take a daily probiotic with at least thirty billion units and twelve strains of bacteria. That will provide you immensely more and better probiotics than yogurt. One bright spot among yogurts is sugar-free coconut milk–based yogurt. It is creamy and delicious without the bad ingredients.

## Exercise Regularly

There are countless studies on the amazing health benefits of exercise and its ability to help prevent, mitigate, and even help reverse disease. Just think about the fact that our bodies are two-thirds water. What happens to water when it sits still for too long in a pond? It gets stagnant, dirty, and filled with bacteria. But running water is fresh and filled with life. When we get the water in our bodies moving through exercise, it refreshes and revives us. It carries oxygen and nutrients to every part of our bodies and carries toxins and cellular waste out.

I realize exercising when you are in the hospital may not always be practical, but to the extent you can, try to move your body every day. If you are at home and physically able, try to exercise three or more times a week and keep your heart rate up for at least thirty minutes. Exercise does not have to feel like punishment. Choose a form you enjoy and can stick with. You can ride a stationary bike in the comfort of your home while watching TV, or walk, run, or bike outside in the fresh air and nature. You can put headphones on and listen to praise music or an inspiring message. Make it enjoyable! To help motivate you, here are some of the incredible benefits to exercise:

**Exercise improves mental attitude and lowers stress.** Exercise produces natural chemicals in our body called endorphins that act as antidepressants and give us a feeling of euphoria, a positive attitude, and lower stress. Exercise also increases neurotransmitters like serotonin and dopamine, which help fight depression and anxiety. Exercise lowers the stress hormone cortisol, which causes us to store fat and increases blood sugar, cholesterol, triglycerides, and blood pressure.

**Exercise prevents heart disease and heart attacks.** Exercise strengthens your heart muscle, so it doesn't have to work as hard. A strong heart beats less often and rests more. An active person's heart beats sixty to seventy times per minute versus eighty or more times per minute for an inactive person. That means an inactive person's heart can beat 29,000 more times a day than an active person's to perform the same job, adding a lot more wear and tear on it. Regular exercise also enlarges coronary arteries and improves blood flow. It lowers blood pressure, triglycerides, and bad cholesterol and raises good cholesterol.

**Exercise improves your immune system.** A key part of our immunity, which fights sickness, viruses, and infections, is the lymphatic system. Lymphatic fluid is so important that the body has three times more lymph than blood. It also removes toxins and cellular waste. When we don't move much, the lymphatic system becomes sluggish, compromising our immune system. Regular aerobic exercise dramatically increases lymphatic flow and your body's immunity.

**Exercise promotes weight loss.** The only way to lose weight is to burn more calories than you take in. Regular exercise helps with weight loss by burning excess calories. Exercise also increases your basal (resting) metabolic rate, so you continue to burn calories even when you are resting! I would encourage you to not just do cardio several times a week for at least thirty minutes, but also do some weight training, if you are able. Muscles burn a lot of calories, so doing some weight training will help you achieve your optimal weight and stay fit and strong.

**Exercise helps rid the body of toxins.** Toxins are released through sweat. That's why sweat stinks. For this reason, the skin has been called the "third kidney."

**Exercise gives you increased energy.** Numerous studies have shown that exercise increases our energy levels and gives us a more positive mood and mindset. This includes people who have medical conditions that cause serious fatigue, like cancer and heart disease.[12]

**Exercise improves sleep.** Charlene Gamaldo, MD, the medical director of Johns Hopkins Center for Sleep, said, "Based on available studies, we have solid evidence that exercise does, in fact, help you fall asleep more quickly and improves sleep quality."[13]

**Exercise alleviates pain.** The endorphins our bodies produce in response to exercise act like natural morphine and have been shown to reduce chronic pain in many people.

# The Jesus School of Healing

PART OF JESUS' ASSIGNMENT on earth was to reveal God to us in living color—His nature, His heart, His will. The Scripture says He was the perfect representation of God (Hebrews 1:3 MSG). Jesus said, "He who has seen Me has seen the Father" (John 14:9), and "I and My Father are one" (John 10:30). He showed us beyond any doubt that it is God's nature and desire to heal because Jesus healed every person who came to Him for healing. Thirteen times in the Scriptures, it says, "Jesus healed them *all*." In this chapter, we are going to glean powerful truths from Jesus' healings that will stir your faith, encourage your heart, and help you on your own journey to healing.

As you read through these stories of healing, keep this verse in the forefront of your mind: "Jesus Christ is the same yesterday, today, and forever" (Hebrews 13:8). These are not just inspiring stories from antiquity when Jesus walked the earth. No, Jesus is the same yesterday, *today*, and *forever*.

He will never change. He healed people in Bible times, and He is still healing people today! Healing and miracles are part of His nature. I believe He has a healing miracle with your name on it!

> And when Jesus went out He saw a great multitude; and *He was moved with compassion for them, and healed their sick.*
>
> Matthew 14:14

> Now as they went out of Jericho, a great multitude followed Him. And behold, two blind men sitting by the road, when they heard that Jesus was passing by, cried out, saying, "Have mercy on us, O Lord, Son of David!" Then the multitude warned them that they should be quiet; but they cried out all the more, saying, "Have mercy on us, O Lord, Son of David!" So Jesus stood still and called them, and said, "What do you want Me to do for you?" They said to Him, "Lord, that our eyes may be opened." So *Jesus had compassion* and *touched their eyes*. And immediately their eyes received sight, and they followed Him.
>
> Matthew 20:29–34

> Now a leper came to Him, imploring Him, kneeling down to Him and saying to Him, "If You are willing, You can make me clean." Then *Jesus, moved with compassion*, stretched out His hand and *touched him*, and said to him, "*I am willing*; be cleansed." As soon as He had spoken, immediately the leprosy left him, and he was cleansed.
>
> Mark 1:40–42

These passages refer to the compassion Jesus had for those He healed. I want you to know God has compassion for you. He cares about what you are going through. You are His child. He is not a distant, impersonal, uncaring God; He is your heavenly Father, and He is right there with you. You may have to walk through some challenges and fight the good fight of faith (we all do), but God's love and compassion are always abounding toward you. The apostle Paul was beaten, stoned and left for dead, shipwrecked three times, imprisoned several times, bitten by a poisonous snake, and suffered many other hardships—all while doing his best to serve God. He confessed that at times he "despaired even of life" (2 Corinthians 1:8). Yet, in the midst of all these trials, he wrote, "I am persuaded that neither death nor life, nor angels nor principalities nor powers, nor things present nor things to come, nor height nor depth, nor any other created thing, shall be able to separate us from the love of God which is in Christ Jesus our Lord" (Romans 8:38–39). Nothing can separate you from God's love and compassion for you.

Two of the verses above also involve the element of *touch*. Jesus touched the blind men's eyes, and they were healed. He touched the leper, and he was healed. There is a powerful transfer that takes place in the spirit realm through touch, which the Bible also refers to as the "laying on of hands." Deuteronomy 34:9 says, "Now Joshua son of Nun was filled with the spirit of wisdom *because Moses had laid his hands on him*." Moses literally transferred wisdom to Joshua by laying hands on him. Matthew 8:14–15 says, "Now when Jesus had come into Peter's house, He saw his wife's mother lying sick with a fever. So *He touched her hand, and the fever left her*." Luke 4:40 says, "When the sun was setting, all those who had any that were sick with various diseases brought them to Him; and *He laid His hands on every one of them* and healed them." Acts 28:8 says, "And it happened that the father of Publius lay sick of a fever and dysentery.

Paul went in to him and prayed, and *he laid his hands on him* and healed him."

Laying on of hands to heal the sick was not just limited to Jesus and His disciples. Jesus said every believer has the power to lay hands on the sick and see them recover: "And these signs will follow *those who believe*: In My name . . . *they will lay hands on the sick, and they will recover*" (Mark 16:17–18). Notice Jesus said, "those who believe." Not just the twelve disciples. Not just pastors, priests, and religious professionals. Not just super Christians. *All believers* in Christ can lay their hands on the sick and transfer miracle-working power into them for healing. This is so because Jesus put His Spirit—the Holy Spirit—inside every believer (1 Corinthians 3:16; 6:19; Romans 8:9). As believers, we have the most powerful force in the universe living inside us. Jesus said in John 14:12, "Most assuredly, I say to you, *he who believes in Me*, the works that I do he will do also; and greater works than these he will do, because I go to My Father." Jesus was saying, "I am going back to heaven, but I will put My Spirit in every believer and they will carry on My ministry and do the same miraculous works I did." So lay your hand on the part(s) of your body that need healing or on your loved one and command healing, wholeness, and restoration in the name of Jesus. God's miracle-working power will flow through you. I should clarify that this doesn't work like a magic wand. Indeed, some people are healed instantly. I have seen countless instant healings of cancer, blindness, deafness, paralysis, and many other diseases. But most of the time, it takes persistence and patience. You shouldn't get discouraged if what I share in this book doesn't work after a few times. Even Jesus Himself had to lay hands on a blind man a second time before he was completely healed:

> Then He came to Bethsaida; and they brought a blind man to Him, and *begged Him to touch him*. So He took the blind man by the hand and led him out of the town. And when He had spit on his eyes and *put His hands on him*, He asked him if he saw anything. And he looked up and said, "I see men like trees, walking." Then *He put His hands on his eyes again* and made him look up. And he was restored and saw everyone clearly.
>
> Mark 8:22–25

I am pretty sure that if Jesus needed to persist and lay hands on this man twice, then we need to persist. Apply the biblical keys and strategies in this book as many times as you need to get the victory. You may not see anything happen at first, maybe not even after many times. But make no mistake: Things are happening in the unseen realm. If you keep persisting, they will eventually manifest in the natural realm.

When I lay hands on the sick, I speak directly to the sickness like I discussed in chapter 3, and I walk in my spiritual authority in Christ, as discussed in chapter 7. Here is a sample of the kinds of things I say:

"I speak to this sickness [name the sickness or condition], and I command it to be removed from this body, in the name of Jesus. Like Jesus cursed the fig tree and it withered and died, I curse this [cancer/virus/whatever the condition is] and command it to wither and die and bear no more fruit, in Jesus' name. I bind, rebuke, cut off, cast out, cancel, and nullify every sickness, disease, infection, and symptom in this body, in Jesus' name. I cover every cell in your body with the healing, restoring, sanctifying blood of the Lord Jesus Christ, and I command healing from the top of your head to the bottom of your feet, in the mighty name of Jesus! Be healed, delivered, restored, and made whole, in Jesus' name."

You may think, *Do I really have the authority to command healing in Jesus' name?* Jesus and His disciples are our role models. We are supposed to imitate what they did (Ephesians 5:1). Jesus said ordinary believers would do the same works He did (John 14:12). He and His disciples walked in their authority and spoke authoritatively to sickness and *commanded* healing. Here are a few examples:

> [Jesus to Peter's mother-in-law:] He stood over her and *rebuked the fever*, and it left her. And immediately she arose and served them.
>
> Luke 4:39

> [Jesus to a leper:] "Be cleansed."
>
> Mark 1:41

> [Jesus] said to the paralytic, "*I say to you, arise, take up your bed, and go to your house.*" Immediately he arose, took up his bed, and went out in the presence of them all.
>
> Mark 2:10–12

> [When Jesus raised a girl from the dead:] Then *He took the child by the hand* [touch], and *said to her*, "Talitha, cumi," which is translated, "*Little girl, I say to you, arise.*" Immediately the girl arose and walked, for she was twelve years of age. And they were overcome with great amazement.
>
> Mark 5:41–42

> Then Peter said, "Silver and gold I do not have, but what I do have I give you: *In the name of Jesus Christ of Nazareth, rise up and walk.*" And he took him by the right hand and lifted him up, and immediately his feet and ankle bones received strength. So, he, leaping up, stood and walked and en-

tered the temple with them—walking, leaping, and praising God.

Acts 3:5–8

Now it came to pass, as Peter went through all parts of the country, that he also came down to the saints who dwelt in Lydda. There he found a certain man named Aeneas, who had been bedridden eight years and was paralyzed. And *Peter said to him, "Aeneas, Jesus the Christ heals you. Arise and make your bed."* Then he arose immediately.

Acts 9:32–34

And in Lystra a certain man without strength in his feet was sitting, a cripple from his mother's womb, who had never walked. This man heard Paul speaking. Paul, observing him intently and seeing that he had faith to be healed, *said with a loud voice, "Stand up straight on your feet!"* And he leaped and walked.

Acts 14:8–10

And Jesus went about all Galilee, teaching in their synagogues, preaching the gospel of the kingdom, and healing *all kinds* of sickness and *all kinds* of disease among the people.

Matthew 4:23

Then Jesus went about all the cities and villages, teaching in their synagogues, preaching the gospel of the kingdom, and healing *every* sickness and *every* disease among the people.

Matthew 9:35

These verses say Jesus healed "all kinds" and "every" sickness and disease. Sometimes people hear something from the doctor or read something online that causes them to believe their particular condition cannot be healed. Perhaps they've never heard of anybody getting healed of that condition. These verses make it clear that God can and does heal every kind of medical condition. He has all power. He spoke the whole universe into existence, parted the Red Sea, and raised Jesus from the dead. He can heal any medical condition under the sun. I shared some astonishing miracles in this book, including that of a person who was raised from the dead, and I have witnessed countless healings of so-called incurable medical conditions.

> Jesus came down the mountain with the cheers of the crowd still ringing in his ears. Then a leper appeared and dropped to his knees before Jesus, praying, "Master, if you want to, you can heal my body." Jesus reached out and touched him, saying, "*I want to*. Be clean." Then and there, all signs of the leprosy were gone.
>
> Matthew 8:1–3 MSG

Jesus told this leper, "I want to." We serve an "I want to" God. He wants to heal you. Sometimes people believe God can heal them but wonder if He really wants to. They have guilt and shame because of the lives they've lived and feel like God may not be too motivated to heal them. Nothing could be further from the truth. Jesus washed away all your sins—past, present, and future. His blood made you totally blameless before God. Forgive yourself of your past mistakes because God forgives you. You are His child, and He loves you more than you can comprehend. Receive His love. Receive His forgiveness. Receive His words down in your spirit: "I want to."

> Now when Jesus had entered Capernaum, a centurion came to Him, pleading with Him, saying, "Lord, my servant is lying

> at home paralyzed, dreadfully tormented." And Jesus said to him, "I will come and heal him." The centurion answered and said, "Lord, I am not worthy that You should come under my roof. But *only speak a word, and my servant will be healed*. . . ." When Jesus heard it, He marveled, and said to those who followed, "Assuredly, I say to you, I have not found such great faith, not even in Israel!" . . . Then Jesus said to the centurion, "Go your way; and *as you have believed, so let it be done for you*." And his servant was healed that same hour.
>
> Matthew 8:5–8, 10, 13

This centurion acknowledged that Jesus did not have to be physically present for His servant to get healed. All He had to do was "speak a word" from a distance. That's because there is no distance in the spirit realm. There is no distance with prayer and declaring the Word of God. If you have a loved one who is sick and you can't be with them physically, know that your prayers and Scripture declarations over them are just as effective.

The second truth from this passage comes from Jesus' words "as you have believed, so let it be done for you." As we examined in chapter 2, Jesus said this phrase to many people He healed. It shows us that God meets us at the level of our faith. What we believe is what we are going to receive from Him. Faith is the currency of heaven. Jesus is saying the same thing to you today: "As you believe, so let it be done for you." Take the limits off and stretch your faith to believe for your miracle!

> He cast out the spirits with a word, and *healed all who were sick*, that it might be fulfilled which was spoken by Isaiah the prophet, saying: "*He Himself took our infirmities and bore our sicknesses*."
>
> Matthew 8:16–17

Notice the phrase "healed *all* who were sick." Jesus healed every person who came to Him for healing. He never denied anyone for any reason. He's "the same yesterday, today, and forever" (Hebrews 13:8). He won't deny you as you seek Him for healing. I'm not saying the healing will come fast or easy. I'm not saying every healing is miraculous; God uses doctors and medicine too. And like I said in chapter 1, I'm not saying everyone gets healed this side of heaven. But it is God's desire to heal, and the healing will come in His way and on His timetable.

The last part of this passage contains one of the greatest truths about healing in the Bible. It says, "He Himself [Jesus] took our infirmities and bore our sicknesses." He *took* them. I repeat: He *took* them. What does that mean? As I covered in chapter 1, it was prophesied in Isaiah 53:4–5 that Jesus would not only take our sins upon Himself at the cross, but take the sicknesses and diseases that came into the world because of Adam and Eve's original sin in the Garden. This verse in Matthew 8:17 affirms this promise in the clearest possible terms when it says Jesus "took our infirmities and bore our sicknesses." First Peter 2:24 adds, "By [His] stripes you *were* healed" (past tense). Jesus paid the price for your healing two thousand years ago when He hung on the cross. He took 39 brutal lashes on his body, a crown of thorns painfully stuck on His head, a spear jabbed in His side, and nails in His hands and feet. He suffered in His body so we might have health in ours. You may be waiting for your healing to manifest, but it has already been paid for with the precious blood of Christ!

> And again He entered Capernaum after some days, and it was heard that He was in the house. Immediately many gathered together, so that there was no longer room to

> receive them, not even near the door. And He preached the word to them. Then they came to Him, bringing a paralytic who was carried by four men. And when they could not come near Him because of the crowd, they uncovered the roof where He was. So when they had broken through, they let down the bed on which the paralytic was lying. *When Jesus saw their faith*, He said to the paralytic, "Son, your sins are forgiven you. . . . I say to you, arise, take up your bed, and go to your house." Immediately he arose, took up the bed, and went out in the presence of them all, so that all were amazed and glorified God, saying, "We never saw anything like this!"
>
> Mark 2:1–5, 11–12

I love this story about four men who brought their paralytic friend to be healed by Jesus. They were so determined to help their friend, when they couldn't get in to see Jesus because of the large crowd, they hoisted him up on the roof, tore a hole in it, and lowered him down in front of Jesus. The passage says, "*When Jesus saw their faith*," He healed the paralytic. First, this tells us that our faith can help a friend or loved one get healed. Even if they are unconscious or can't exercise their own faith for some reason, God will respond to *our* faith. Second, as discussed in chapter 2, God cares about our needs, but He responds to our faith. The healing came when Jesus *saw their faith*. Faith is what gets God's attention and moves Him to act.

A similar passage is found in Acts 14:8–10:

> And in Lystra a certain man without strength in his feet was sitting, a cripple from his mother's womb, who had never walked. *This man heard Paul speaking*. Paul, observing him intently and *seeing that he had faith to be healed*, said with

> a loud voice, "Stand up straight on your feet!" And he leaped and walked.

Like the story above about Jesus healing the paralytic when He saw their faith, this verse says Paul healed a crippled man after "*seeing that he had faith to be healed.*" Can God see your faith? Can He see you praying faith-filled prayers and declaring His Word over yourself or a loved one in faith? If so, you can rest assured He will respond.

This story about Paul healing the crippled man also says, "This man heard Paul speaking." The Bible says faith comes by hearing and hearing by the Word of God (Romans 10:17). When you hear good preaching or a testimony about someone who got healed, it stirs your faith. When this man heard Paul preaching, it sparked his faith to receive his healing. Try to feed your faith every day by listening to preaching messages online or on Christian television and reading God's Word. This will keep your faith strong and pave the way for you to receive your miracle.

> While He spoke these things to them, behold, a ruler came and worshiped Him, saying, "My daughter has just died, but come and lay Your hand on her and she will live." So Jesus arose and followed him, and so did His disciples. And suddenly, a woman who had a flow of blood for twelve years came from behind and touched the hem of His garment. For *she said to herself, "If only I may touch His garment, I shall be made well."* But Jesus turned around, and when He saw her He said, "Be of good cheer, daughter; *your faith has made you well.*" And the woman was made well from that hour.
>
> Matthew 9:18–22

This woman "said to herself, 'If only I may touch His garment, I *shall* be made well.'" Not "Maybe I'll be healed." Not "I've tried everything; I might as well try this." No, she said, "I *shall* be made well." She had a resolute, determined faith, and she verbalized it. In the original Greek of the New Testament, this verse is in the continuous tense, so it should read, "She *kept on* saying to herself . . ." Over and over, she declared that she would be healed if she touched Jesus' garment. I covered the power of our words extensively in chapter 3, but I want to encourage you to use your words to speak what you want. Jesus said in Mark 11:23, "Whoever . . . does not doubt in his heart, but believes that those things he says will be done, *he will have whatever he says*." This is an extravagant promise, but I have seen it manifested in my own life countless times and those to whom I have ministered. The lady in this passage with the issue of blood is also proof. She repeatedly declared out of her mouth that she would be healed when she touched Jesus' garment, and that is exactly what happened.

The other truth comes from the phrase "*your faith has made you well*." Jesus repeated different iterations of this phrase to many people He healed. The principle is clear: God will meet us at the level of our faith. It is great to have lots of people praying for us, but in the end our own faith will determine what we receive from God. A few verses later, Jesus repeats this principle again to two blind men:

> When Jesus departed from there, two blind men followed Him, crying out and saying, "Son of David, have mercy on us!" And when He had come into the house, the blind men came to Him. And Jesus said to them, "*Do you believe that I am able to do this?*" They said to Him, "Yes, Lord." Then

> He touched their eyes, saying, "*According to your faith let it be to you.*" And their eyes were opened.
>
> Matthew 9:27–30

Jesus asked the two blind men if they believed He was able to heal them. He is asking you the same question: Do you believe He is able to heal you completely and make you whole? Faith is the currency of heaven; it is how we receive anything from God. James 1:6–7 (NIV) says, "But when you ask, you must believe and not doubt, because the one who doubts is like a wave of the sea, blown and tossed by the wind. *That person should not expect to receive anything from the Lord.*" So believing God is a prerequisite to receiving your healing or anything else from Him. When these two men answered Jesus that they believed, their miracle came. Notice the reference to touch again: He touched their eyes. He then repeated the principle: "According to your faith let it be done to you."

> And He came down with them and stood on a level place with a crowd of His disciples and a great multitude of people from all Judea and Jerusalem, and from the seacoast of Tyre and Sidon, who came to hear Him and be healed of their diseases. . . . And the whole multitude *sought to touch Him, for power went out from Him and healed them all.*
>
> Luke 6:17, 19

This is another reference to touch. The people sought to touch Jesus because supernatural healing power was transferred from Him through touch. Jesus said every believer in Christ has this same ability. In Mark 16:17–18, He said, "These signs will follow *those who believe*: In My name . . . *they will lay hands on the sick and they will recover.*" Are you a believer? Then, according to Jesus, supernatural signs should follow you and you can lay hands on the sick and see them recover. But you must believe for it. The promise is only for "those who believe." Nothing happens without faith. Jesus added in John 14:12, "Most assuredly, I say to you, *he who believes in Me*, the works that I do he will do also; and greater works than these he will do, because I go to My Father." Do you believe you can do the same supernatural works Jesus did? Either we believe what Jesus said or we don't. I'm asking you to be a believer and not a doubter. Dare to believe you can lay your hands on your own sick body or someone else's and see them recover. You might never have been taught these verses or concepts before, but you can take Jesus at His word. I have seen the truth of these verses manifested in my own life for over 25 years as I have laid hands on the sick, and I have seen God use many other ordinary believers to do the same.

> Then He called His twelve disciples together and gave them power and authority over all demons, and *to cure diseases*. He sent them to preach the kingdom of God and *to heal the sick*.
>
> Luke 9:1–2

> After these things the Lord appointed *seventy others* also, and sent them two by two before His face into every city and place where He Himself was about to go. . . . "And *heal the sick* there, and say to them, 'The kingdom of God has come near to you.'"
>
> Luke 10:1, 9

> And these signs will follow *those who believe*: In My name . . . *they will lay hands on the sick and they will recover*.
>
> Mark 16:17–18

These three verses show a fascinating progression. First, Jesus was the only one healing the sick. Then He sent His twelve disciples out and gave them power and authority to cure diseases and commissioned them to "heal the sick" (Luke 9:1–2). In Matthew 10:8, Jesus gave them an even more audacious instruction: "Heal the sick, cleanse the lepers, raise the dead, cast out demons." Some theologians and churches teach that this power and authority were only for Jesus and His disciples, and that miraculous healing went away after the apostolic era. This teaching is patently erroneous and easy to disprove biblically and experientially. Not only did Jesus instruct the Twelve to heal the sick, He then broadened it out to seventy more followers, whom He also instructed to "heal the sick" (Luke 10:1, 9). After these seventy, He broadened it out further to *every believer*. In Mark 16:17–18, He said supernatural signs would follow "those who believe," one of which is "they will lay hands on the sick and they will recover." He added in John 14:12, "Most assuredly, I say to you, he who believes in Me, the works that I do he will do also; and greater works than these he will do, because I go to My Father." Every believer has the same Holy Spirit in them who empowered Jesus and His disciples to do the miraculous works they did. Every believer can minister healing to themselves and others. All it takes is faith to believe it.

> Now as Jesus passed by, He saw a man who was blind from birth. And His disciples asked Him, saying, "Rabbi, who sinned, this man or his parents, that he was born blind?" Jesus answered, "*Neither this man nor his parents sinned, but that the works of God should be revealed in him.* I must work the works of Him who sent Me while it is day; the night is coming when no one can work. As long as I am in

> the world, I am the light of the world." When He had said these things, He spat on the ground and made clay with the saliva; and He anointed the eyes of the blind man with the clay. And He said to him, "*Go, wash in the pool of Siloam*" (which is translated, Sent). So he went and washed, and came back seeing.
>
> John 9:1–7

Jesus' disciples assumed this man's blindness was caused by either his own sin or his parents'. Some Christians have been taught that God puts sickness on people to punish them, but that is absolutely false doctrine. Jesus corrects this erroneous thinking and tells His disciples that the sickness was not a result of any sin, "but that the works of God should be revealed in him." God does not put sickness on people for any reason, but when sickness happens, He will use it to reveal His works and glorify Himself. Jesus said the same thing before He raised Lazarus from the dead: "This sickness is not unto death, but for the glory of God" (John 11:4). An obvious way God gets glory out of sickness is when He miraculously heals people, but that's not the only way. He gets glory when you stay in faith, keep a good attitude, and keep praising Him while you are waiting for healing. That's a witness to others. He gets glory when your sickness causes you to press into Him more, develop your spiritual muscles, and become more dangerous to the enemy. Powerful, dangerous (to the enemy) Christians are forged in the fire of adversity. He gets glory when a body of believers and family members unite to rally around someone who is sick. He gets glory when family members set aside their differences and become reconciled because of a loved one's illness. I am a big believer in Romans 8:28: "All things work together for good to those who love God, to those who are the called according to His purpose." It doesn't say all things *are* good; it says all things *work together for* good. If you stay in faith, God will work this sickness for your good, bring you out better than you were before, and use it to glorify Himself.

The other great truth from this passage comes from Jesus putting clay on this blind man's eyes and then instructing him to "go, wash in the pool of Siloam." When the man obeyed the instruction, his healing came. Sometimes your miracle is in an instruction. When you seek God daily and endeavor to listen to His still, small voice (1 Kings 19:12), He will give you valuable instructions in your spirit. Your miracle may be contained in an instruction and will manifest when you obey that instruction. Like this man, it may be a very simple, practical instruction.

My wife and I tried for three years to have our second child to no avail. We thought we just couldn't have any more children. Of course, we prayed and declared and did everything I talk about in this book, but nothing worked. One day, she watched a show on Daystar Christian network, and the guest talked about how being low in progesterone can prevent some women from getting pregnant. They offered a progesterone cream for sale. My wife knew in her spirit that God orchestrated for her to watch this show and was prompting her to get that cream. Shortly after using the cream, she became pregnant with our second child. The miracle was in the instruction.

# Faith Builders

THIS CHAPTER CONTAINS short devotions on faith that are meant to build your faith and encourage your heart. Meditate on (ponder, mull over) each one individually and let it percolate past your mind down to your spirit. Proverbs 18:14 says, "The spirit of a man will sustain him in sickness." I pray these devotionals will nourish and strengthen your spirit. Stay in faith and keep your eyes on Jesus . . . your breakthrough is on the way!

## 1

> Now faith is the *assurance* (*title deed*, confirmation) of things hoped for (*divinely guaranteed*), and the *evidence of things not seen [the conviction of their reality*—faith comprehends as *fact* what cannot be experienced by the physical senses].
>
> Hebrews 11:1 AMP

This translation of Hebrews 11:1 is such an amazing and thorough definition of Bible faith. Faith is believing that we have the *title deed* to things God promised us and being so convinced of their reality that they are already a *fact* in our minds, even though they haven't manifested in the physical realm yet. The world says you have to see it to believe it, but faith says you have to believe first before you'll see it come to pass.

A perfect example in the Bible is when God promised Abraham that he and Sarah would have a child when Abraham was 75 years old, and Sarah was well past her childbearing years. That promise took 25 years to come to pass, making Abraham around one hundred years old when he and Sarah had Isaac. Sometimes God will wait until a situation is so impossible that only He gets the credit and glory for it. Not only were Abraham and Sarah impossibly old to have a child, but 25 years is an excruciatingly long time to wait. Most people would not have had the faith to believe this promise in the first place, much less have hung in there for 25 years. But Abraham's faith is a model for us all.

Romans 4:19–21 says, "And not being weak in faith, *he did not consider his own body*, already dead (since he was about a hundred years old), and the deadness of Sarah's womb. *He did not waver* at the promise of God through unbelief, but was strengthened in faith, giving glory to God, and being *fully convinced* that what He had promised He was also able to perform."

Notice that Abraham did not consider his body, which was as good as dead. That's exactly what you need to do. Don't consider you or your loved one's sick body in the natural. That means don't focus on the natural circumstances. Don't obsess on what the doctor said. Don't be persuaded by what things look like in the natural. Sometimes you have to turn off your mind because your mind can be too influenced by the natural facts. I'm not telling you to deny the facts, but to realize that God is not limited by the facts. He's a supernatural God. Like Abraham, be *fully convinced* that God will keep His promises. One touch from God can turn your whole situation around.

## 2

> [Jesus talking:] "If you can believe, *all* things are possible to him who believes."
>
> Mark 9:23

This is an extravagant promise that shows the incredible power of faith. Jesus said *all* things—not *some* things, not *most* things, but *all* things—are possible if we have the faith to believe for it. He didn't say if you can figure it out, if you're a good enough person, or if you ask Him enough times. He said *just believe*. Basically, Jesus was giving us a blank check if we have the faith for something. We either believe Jesus and take Him at His word—or we don't. Our own faith sets the limits of what we receive from God. Take the limits off and stretch your faith to believe God for your miracle. He has all power, and nothing is impossible with Him!

## 3

> [Jesus talking:] "Whatever you ask in prayer, believe that you *have received* it [past tense], and it *will be* yours [future tense]."
>
> Mark 11:24 ESV

This is another extravagant, blank-check promise from Jesus that depends on our faith. He said when we pray for something, we need to believe we *already have it* (past tense). We may not have it in the physical realm yet, but we have to believe we have it in the spiritual realm because God promised it to us. I like to say we have it in our faith account. Hebrews 11:1, which we looked at above, says we have to be fully convinced that we have the title deed to what God promised us, and we have to keep on believing it no matter what things look like in the natural. Jesus said if we do that, we *will*—not *may* or *probably* or *there's a good chance*—but we *will* have the things we have asked for.

## 4

> But let him *ask in faith*, with *no doubting*, for he who doubts is like a wave of the sea driven and tossed by the wind. *For let not that man suppose he will receive anything from the Lord.*
>
> James 1:6–7

The two previous verses said we can have anything if we have the faith for it. This verse is the flip side. It says if we doubt, we can't expect to receive anything from God. It also says when we doubt, we are like a wave of the sea tossed around. Don't be tossed around by your emotions, the enemy's lies, doubt, fear, or defeated mindsets. Believe God over anyone or anything else. Take steps every day to feed your faith and keep it strong, as I laid out in chapter 2. When you do that, there won't be room for faith-robbing thoughts to take root in your mind.

## 5

> [Jesus talking:] "Have faith in God. For assuredly, I say to you, whoever *says* to this mountain, 'Be removed and be cast into the sea,' and *does not doubt in his heart, but believes* that those things he *says* will be done, he will have whatever he says."
>
> Mark 11:22–23

Jesus was hungry and saw a fig tree from a distance, but when He got up to it, there were no figs on the tree. The Scripture says He "cursed" the fig tree, or spoke negatively to it. The next morning, His disciples were astonished when they saw the tree had withered and died. They asked Jesus how He did that. Instead of saying, "Because I am God and I have all power," He responded with the above passage. His message was clear: "If you have faith in God, you have this same power in your mouth. You can command a mountain to be removed, and you can have whatever things you say." Proverbs 18:21 adds that "death and life are in the power of the tongue."

You have the power in your own mouth to speak to that sickness and command it to go in Jesus' name! You have the power to speak death over cancer, diseases, viruses, infections, and other medical conditions attacking your body, just like Jesus cursed the fig tree and it died. When I pray for sick people, I say something like, "I curse this [cancer or name the condition] and command it to wither and die and bear no more fruit, in the mighty name of Jesus. I command this [name of condition] to be removed from this body right now in Jesus' name and never return."

It is no coincidence that Jesus referred to a mountain to represent our challenges. Mountains look immovable, like they will never change. They are huge, intimidating, and daunting. Jesus wanted us to know that faith-filled words have the power to move even mountains. It's not enough just to pray about the mountain, have faith that the mountain will move, or have positive thoughts about the mountain. Don't beg God to move the mountain. Don't complain to your friends about the mountain. Jesus told us to *speak to* our mountains and *command* them to go!

## 6

Without faith it is *impossible* to please [God].

Hebrews 11:6

This shows us how important faith is to God. We can do a lot of good things, but if we don't have faith, it is impossible to please Him.

## 7

The just shall *live* by faith.

Hebrews 10:38

Faith is not just an optional accessory in our life or something we pull out only in a crisis. God says we are to *live* by faith. That means He wants us to use our faith every day and believe Him for everything we need. Faith gives us access to supernatural power, healing, provision, and other blessings not available without faith.

## 8

We walk by faith, not by sight.

2 Corinthians 5:7

This verse means we don't go by what we see in the natural. Faith is believing in what we cannot see. If you can see it or figure it out, it doesn't require faith. You or your loved one's situation may look really bad—even hopeless—in the natural, but you can't be moved by that. God is not limited by the natural. He's a supernatural God. There is always hope with God because He can do the impossible. I have prayed for many people who were on life support and made a miraculous turnaround, some even after the family had disconnected the machine. I have trained myself over the years not to be moved by how bad a patient looks in the natural. One touch from God can turn any situation around. It's never over until God says it's over!

## 9

By [faith], the elders obtained a good testimony.

Hebrews 11:2

All the testimonies of miracles in the Bible, and every one in modern times, happened because of faith. Faith in God and His promises is how you or your loved one will obtain a good testimony from this health situation.

## 10

Do not become sluggish, but imitate those who through *faith and patience* inherit the promises.

Hebrews 6:12

Notice how it takes both faith and patience to inherit the promises of God. Faith is not a magic wand that always yields instant results. We need patience, too. It took 25 years after God promised Abraham an heir for the promise to come to pass. It took forty years for the vision God gave Moses of delivering the Israelites to be fulfilled. It took seventeen years in captivity for the dreams God gave Joseph to come to pass. I am not saying your healing is going to take years, but you need patience and persistence to receive the promises of God. They don't all come quickly and easily.

## 11

> [Jesus to Simon Peter:] "Simon, Simon! Indeed, Satan has asked for you, that he may sift you as wheat. But I have prayed for you, that your faith should not fail."
>
> Luke 22:31–32

Jesus did not say He would pray for Peter to be delivered from adversity. All of us are going to experience adversity. God is not going to save us from every trial. But Jesus prayed that Peter's faith would not fail. That's because faith is the most valuable asset we have. It takes faith to access everything God has for us. As long as we have faith, we can turn any situation around.

## 12

> In this you greatly rejoice, though now for a little while, if need be, you have been grieved by various trials, that the genuineness of your faith, *being much more precious than gold* that perishes, though it is tested by fire, may be found to praise, honor, and glory at the revelation of Jesus Christ.
>
> 1 Peter 1:6–7

Anybody can have faith when they are standing on the mountaintop with good health, plenty of money in the bank, and everything going their way. Anybody can have faith when they are in church surrounded by their friends, singing praise songs with the worship team, and listening to an encouraging message from the pastor. But the true quality of our faith comes out when we face trials. Every person's faith will be tested by trials in life. We will never know what kind of faith we have until it is put to the test. Stay strong and pass the test, and your breakthrough will come!

Notice also that it says your faith is more precious than gold. You can lose gold, lose material things, lose your health. But if you have faith, you can get all those things back.

## 13

"Lord, I believe; help my unbelief!"

Mark 9:24

This verse comes from a story about a man whose son was mute and had seizures. Jesus told the man, "If you can believe, all things are possible to him who believes" (Mark 9:23). I love the honesty and vulnerability of the man's response to Jesus: "Lord, I believe; help my unbelief" (Mark 9:24). If we are honest, all of us struggle with some unbelief from time to time, especially when we're going through a long, hard trial and don't see anything changing. None of us has perfect faith. The great thing is, God is okay with that. He doesn't expect us to have perfect faith. He has grace and mercy on us when our faith is weak. Jesus didn't rebuke this man for his unbelief. He didn't say, "Since you have some unbelief, forget it. I'm not going to heal your son." No, Jesus had compassion and healed the son.

This reminds me of the story of Peter walking on the water. The disciples were in a boat crossing the Sea of Galilee at night when they encountered Jesus walking on the water next to their boat. At first, they weren't sure it was Jesus; they thought it might be a ghost. Peter said, "Lord, if it is You, command me to come to You on the water" (Matthew 14:28). Jesus said, "Come" (Matthew 14:29). Then Peter did what no person has ever done before or since. By faith, he stepped out of the boat and started walking on the water. But moments later, the wind and waves got very boisterous, and Peter became afraid. He began to sink in the water. Jesus didn't say, "Too bad, Peter. You shouldn't have gotten afraid. You should have kept your faith. I'm going to let you drown." No, Jesus reached out His hand to Peter and lifted him up (Matthew 14:31). Whenever you feel weak in your faith, know that Jesus is reaching His hand out to lift you up. He doesn't judge you. He's not disappointed in you. He loves you, and He's full of mercy and grace.

# Notes

### Chapter 1 Key 1: God Is a Healer

1. Based on *Ellicott's Commentary for English*, *MacLaren's Expositions*, *Cambridge Bible for Schools and Colleges*, and *Barnes Notes on the Bible* (all accessed at https://biblehub.com/commentaries/isaiah/53-4.htm), as well as the Complete Jewish Bible and Young's Literal Translation.

### Chapter 2 Key 2: Unleashing the Power of Faith

1. Dwight L. Moody. AZQuotes.com, Wind and Fly LTD, 2022. https://www.azquotes.com/quote/867872, accessed March 10, 2022.
2. Prophecy about Jesus.

### Chapter 4 Key 4: Prayer That Works

1. Martin Luther, quoted at Goodreads, accessed March 26, 2022, www.goodreads.com/quotes/653583.
2. Oswald Chambers, quoted at OverallMotivation, accessed March 26, 2022, www.overallmotivation.com/quotes/oswald-chambers-quotes-prayer-faith-fear.

### Chapter 5 Key 5: Praise Precedes the Victory

1. "12-Year-Old Drowns and His Sister Sings Him Back to Life," *The 700 Club*, accessed July 8, 2022, https://www1.cbn.com/12-year-old-drowns-and-his-sister-sings-him-back-life.
2. Ralph F. Wilson, "74: The Thankful Leper (Luke 17:11–19)," JesusWalk, accessed March 26, 2022, www.jesuswalk.com/luke/074-thankful-leper.htm.

3. Doug Hershey, "The True Meaning of Shalom," Fellowship of Israel Related Ministries, January 3, 2020, https://firmisrael.org/learn/the-meaning-of-shalom.

4. In Old Testament times, balm of Gilead was a medical ointment for the healing of wounds. This verse is a prophetic reference to Jesus as our Healer.

### Chapter 6 Key 6: Healing the Soul

1. There is no one verse that defines the soul in the Bible, but the 432 verses that mention the soul make it clear that it is the seat of our mind, will, and emotions.

2. "The Effects of Stress on Your Body," WebMD, October 15, 2020, www.webmd.com.

3. Caroline Leaf, *Who Switched Off My Brain?: Controlling Toxic Thoughts and Emotions* (New York: Thomas Nelson, 2009), 4.

### Chapter 8 Key 8: Taking Care of Your Temple

1. Chris Wark, *Chris Beat Cancer: A Comprehensive Plan for Healing Naturally* (New York: Hay House, 2018).

2. Cole Kazdin, "The Culinary Revolution Has Come for Hospitals," *The Paper Gown* (blog), October 10, 2018, https://thepapergown.zocdoc.com/the-culinary-revolution-has-come-for-hospitals.

3. Jane Hurst, "8 Things to Know about Eating Healthy in the Hospital," Healthcare in America, August 21, 2018, https://healthcareinamerica.us/8-things-to-know-about-eating-healthy-in-the-hospital-402a1aa48089.

4. Leah Zerbe, "Bad News for Your Brain: Artificially Sweetened Drinks Increase Risk of Stroke and Dementia," Dr. Axe, April 26, 2017, https://draxe.com/health/artificially-sweetened-drinks-increase-risk-of-stroke-and-dementia/.

5. Joseph Mercola, *Effortless Healing: 9 Simple Ways to Sidestep Illness, Shed Excess Weight, and Help Your Body Fix Itself* (New York: Harmony Books, 2015), 17.

6. "Eat Fruits and Vegetables for a Long Life," Harvard Health Publishing, Harvard Medical School, March 13, 2014, https://www.health.harvard.edu/staying-healthy/eat-fruits-and-veggies-for-a-long-life.

7. Ron Elli, "Study Found That Fruits and Vegetable Diet May Reduce Risk of Death," Mexico Bariatric Center, April 4, 2014, https://mexicobariatriccenter.com/study-fruits-vegetable-diet-reduce-risk-death.

8. Mark Hyman, "Eat Your Medicine: Food as Pharmacology," Dr. Hyman, accessed March 17, 2022, https://drhyman.com/blog/2011/10/14/eat-your-medicine-food-as-pharmacology.

9. Mark Hyman, *Food: What the Heck Should I Eat?* (New York: Little, Brown & Company, 2018), 28, 78.

10. Leah Zerbe, "Dirty Dozen List: Are You Eating the Most Pesticide-Laden Produce?" Dr. Axe, March 25, 2020, https://draxe.com/health/dirty-dozen.

11. "Dirty Dozen: EWG's 2022 Shopper's Guide to Pesticides in Produce," accessed July 7, 2022, https://www.ewg.org/foodnews/dirty-dozen.php. Copyright © Environmental Working Group. Reproduced with permission.

12. Jennifer Warner, "Exercise Fights Fatigue, Boosts Energy," WebMD, November 3, 2006, https://www.webmd.com/diet/news/20061103/exercise-fights-fatigue-boosts-energy.

13. Charlene Gamaldo, quoted in "Exercising for Better Sleep," Johns Hopkins Medicine, accessed October 8, 2020, https://www.hopkinsmedicine.org/health/wellness-and-prevention/exercising-for-better-sleep.

**Steve Austin** was a young attorney minding his own business when God changed his life forever and ignited a fire in him to see people healed. He went on two foreign mission trips—one to India and the other to Egypt—where he experienced God in ways he never had before and witnessed astonishing miracles. In an instant, God healed people of blindness, deafness, paralysis, cancer, and all kinds of diseases—just like we read about in the Bible. The small religious box he had put God in was shattered, and he could never go back to casual Sunday Christianity and powerless religion. God is still doing miracles today, healing people and setting them free, and Steve wanted to be a part of what He was doing.

Steve came back from those trips a changed person, and God began to call him out of practicing law into full-time ministry. Steve has been a pastor at Lakewood Church in Houston, Texas, the largest church in America, for 20 years. For the past 25 years, he has been ministering to the sick—first as a volunteer, then as a pastor—in the largest medical center in the world—the Texas Medical Center in Houston, Texas. He has always wished he had a book he could give patients that would equip them spiritually to win the battle for their health. He searched every book on healing but could never find what he was looking for, so he decided to write his own. *God Heals* is a compilation of everything he's learned about healing over many years of ministering to countless sick people and their families.

Through the years, Steve also observed that most hospital patients and their families do not get the spiritual care they need, which he believes is as important as the medical care. So he set out to create a ministry that would meet this critical need. In 2021, after completing chaplaincy training at MD Anderson Cancer Center, he launched Living Hope Chaplaincy, a 501(c)(3) nonprofit organization that puts teams of trained volunteers in hospitals to provide spiritual care to patients, patients' families, and health-care workers. His dream is to have teams in hospitals across America and internationally. You can visit the website at www.livinghopechaplaincy.org and follow Living Hope Chaplaincy on Facebook and Instagram.

Steve could not do what he does without the love and support of his amazing wife of almost 28 years, Suzie. They have two wonderful daughters, Lindsey and Lauren, and everybody's favorite family member—a sweet Maltipoo named Lulu. You can follow him on his personal Facebook page and two Facebook groups he created: God Heals, where he shares encouragement for people battling sickness and where people can post their prayer requests; and Healthy You, which has daily health and wellness tips and recipes.

@SteveAustin111

@groups/874985123314528

@groups/realhealthyyou